A Literary Feast

A Literary Feast

Recipes and Writings by American Women
Authors from History

Edited by Yvonne Schofer

**JONES
BOOKS**

Madison, Wisconsin

Copyright © 2003 Friends of the University of Wisconsin-Madison Libraries
All rights reserved

Jones Books
309 N. Hillside Terrace
Madison, Wisconsin 53705-3328
www.jonesbooks.com

First edition, first printing

ISBN 0-9721217-2-2

Printed in the United States of America

Excerpts from *An Army Doctor's Wife on the Frontier,* by Emily FitzGerald, edited by Abe Laufe, © 1962 by University of Pittsburgh Press, are reprinted by permission of the University of Pittsburgh Press.

Library of Congress Cataloging-in-Publication Data

A literary feast : recipes and writings by American women authors from
history / edited by Yvonne Schofer.— 1st ed.
     p. cm.
  Includes bibliographical references and index.
  ISBN 0-9721217-1-4 (hardcover : alk. paper)
  1. Cookery. 2. Literary cookbooks. I. Schofer, Yvonne, 1939-
  TX714.L567 2003
  641.5—dc21

                            2003013855

Table of Contents

Introduction

Cooking has changed a great deal since the nineteenth century. Ovens have temperature controls; water comes from faucets located right in kitchens; fruits and vegetables are available in all seasons, and you no longer have to pluck your chickens before roasting them. Refrigerators can keep leftovers fresh for days and microwaves can reheat them in minutes. None of these conveniences existed a hundred years ago. But while the methods of cooking have changed radically over the last century, the central importance of food in day-to-day life remains constant. And what better way to understand that importance than through the recipes of an era? This cookbook provides an abundance of such recipes from the nineteenth century, along with excerpts from American literature written by women (who were, after all, the primary cooks of the time) that further illustrate where food and eating fit into domestic life. Together they provide an unusual—and entertaining—snapshot of the world of an earlier era.

We first conceived this book a few years ago to highlight texts found in the William B. Cairns Collection of American Women Writers (1650–1920), established in 1979 and housed in the Department of Special Collections, Memorial Library, at the University of Wisconsin–Madison. From the novels, poetry, plays, and essays in the collection, written by mostly nineteenth-century women, it was easy to search and find references to food, meals, and conversations about food. The idea of matching this so-called "food-talk" with recipes of the period, also written by women, soon followed. Cookbooks could serve as a realistic backdrop to literature, which in turn enriched the practical contents of such recipe books by presenting an imaginative picture of domestic life and habits in the nineteenth century.

Although sometimes difficult to achieve, given the abundance of material available, this choice worked well. The process of searching and selecting revealed a great deal about the preparation of meals, the importance of food, the priorities of consumption, the dependence on servants, the inefficiency of primitive kitchens, the seasonal nature of the food supply, and the social settings in which food was prepared and served. Naturally, the perspective from which the authors wrote novels and recipes differed greatly from that of modern readers with their gadget-oriented kitchens. Cooking, and indeed housekeeping in general, was back-breaking work at a time when the wood-stoves, water brought in from outdoor pumps, and undependable food supplies presented homemakers with endless challenges.

Many novels refer to cooking and food and provide glimpses of the enormous amount of work required to prepare and serve the elaborate meals of the period. The day began early with huge breakfasts, which, in the country, would be cooked only after feeding and milking the livestock. Beyond meal preparation, baking was universally performed two or three times a week, each round a twenty-four-hour undertaking. Food had to be preserved and put by for the winter and to prevent spoilage. Special dishes and delicacies invariably accompanied social activities, and many references had regional associations. Commonly mentioned dishes, for example, included those associated with New England: baked beans, brown bread, Indian pudding. Pies and cakes were extremely important; vegetables and salads were rarely discussed. Breads were a staple, as were preserves and "potted meats." Sumptuous holiday celebrations, particularly Thanksgiving, Christmas, and Election Day, yielded both lyrical descriptions in novels and a wealth of recipes.

The Cairns authors, particularly in the early half of the nineteenth century, had high-minded purposes. They wanted to instruct and inspire their readers—but chose to play down the drudgery of the domestic experience. Fortunately for middle-class women, even modest households had servants: on the frontier in the 1840s, Caroline Kirkland in Michigan and Juliette Kinzie in Wisconsin looked for domestic help as soon as they settled in their pioneer homes. In 1870, Emily FitzGerald in Alaska brought a girl from home to help with the cooking and look after the children. The "servant problem" remained a frequent theme in the novels and essays of the second half of the century.

Since the readership was largely female, women's best-selling fiction from the second half of the nineteenth century tends to reflect the concerns of their audience, describing and celebrating domestic ritual. Novels also set the standards by which women were encouraged, if not required, to measure their lives. The cult of the domestic sphere meant that, safely removed from the evil and crassness of the world of business and commerce in which

American men had to participate, women could devote themselves to their civilizing and Christianizing mission, angels in the home, caring for their children and attending to all needs, beginning with those of the household. Of course, women had done that all along, but as domestic tasks became more and more removed from the actual economic sphere in an age of rapid industrialization, they came to be seen not as work but as a natural extension of a woman's role in the world. Domesticity itself became a virtue higher than any other calling. This view informs much of women's fiction. Housekeeping, as described in those works, is a long series of chores, but it paves the way to godliness through order and cleanliness in an ideally seamless web. Food preparation figures prominently in this ideal. While there are few references to daily cooking in the diaries and journals kept by women in the earlier period, the novels of the 1860s and later frequently refer to food and meals.

Many women writers wrote books of advice that attempted to organize and simplify the routines, while also enlarging the domestic sphere by touching on matters of health and education. As early as the 1840s, the vision of woman as moral guardian informs the works of Catharine Beecher (sister of Harriet Beecher Stowe), who wrote over thirty books including *A Treatise on Domestic Economy* and *Domestic Receipts,* which went into many printings over a period of ten years. That vision is also strong in the moral and historical novels of Elizabeth Stuart Phelps and Catharine Maria Sedgwick, who wrote best-sellers at mid-century. A writer such as Susan Warner, the author of the phenomenally successful *The Wide, Wide World,* vividly evokes in her fiction the materiality of nineteenth-century life in America. The Christian heroine's duty not only requires her to prepare generous meals as a mark of her love for those around her, but also to exercise diligence and thrift at all times as part of the divine mission. The setting of food preparation can sometimes become a powerful metaphor: the chaos in Dinah's kitchen at the St. Clares' New Orleans house in *Uncle Tom's Cabin* symbolically represents the moral disorder at the core of slavery.

Some authors expressed their ideas about the education of children through references to food. In *Eight Cousins,* Louisa May Alcott's twelve-year-old heroine Rose Campbell is made, a little reluctantly, to change her diet by her guardian uncle, a doctor with radical ideas about education and nutrition: enervating breakfast coffee will be replaced by wholesome milk and oatmeal, hot biscuits for tea are abandoned in favor of brown bread. Along with these changes comes the removal of Rose's tight leather belt, to the detriment of the tiny waist favored by the fashions of the time; her silk dress will be exchanged for wool in the winter, with an injunction to run around the garden and participate in her male cousins' outdoor activities: girls should be as strong as boys.

Alcott's fiction also stresses the importance of early instruction for girls in the preparation of nutritious food. In *Little Women,* the March girls learn a hard lesson when they prepare and serve a disastrous dinner during Marmee's day off—taken to teach them just that lesson. In a sequel, *Little Men,* Jo surprises her little niece Daisy with the wonderful gift of a miniature kitchen, complete with an irresistible stove. It is not all play, however, and although the initial results are of a halting nature, Daisy's cooking lessons have begun.

In view of these concerns and their overriding importance in the minds of writers, it is no surprise that many authored and published both literary works and cookbooks. Julia McNair Wright was a phenomenally prolific writer whose works ranged from fiction to poetry, religious tracts, temperance writings, cookbooks, and works of botany. Mary Virginia Hawes Terhune was also a novelist and chronicler of household affairs, who wrote under the pseudonym Marion Harland. Her fiction includes twenty-five novels and three volumes of short stories. Having had to overcome practical difficulties in her own housekeeping and cooking early in her marriage, she wanted other women to have the benefit of her experience. Her *Common Sense in the Kitchen* became a best-seller, and was followed by many books dealing with domestic matters.

When cooking schools developed in large cities in the late 1860s and 1870s, their purpose was to help immigrants learn proper American cooking and to train young women for domestic service. However, young middle-class women also became interested in the movement toward scientific cookery, in its attempt to dignify and elevate cooking to the level of a scientific discipline, rejecting the ever-threatening traditional unruliness of kitchen routines in favor of a laboratory approach to food production. Cookbooks generated by the cooking schools became very popular. In the early decades of the twentieth century, many recipes tended to emphasize appearance over nutrition and taste, regrettably promoting the sort of blandness that until recently was the hallmark of much American cooking.

The search for recipes started with the Cairns Collection, providing one of the earliest cookbooks, Eliza Leslie's *Seventy-five Receipts for Pastry, Cakes, and Sweetmeats,* published in 1827 and going through eleven editions to 1839, the date of our copy, a slim volume accompanied by an envelope full of handwritten recipes. Such notes were often tucked in other cookbooks, many of which also display handwritten annotations, stains, and other evidence that they were well used. The historical cookbook collection at Steenbock Library, another University of Wisconsin–Madison library, provided other excellent sources, such as the cooking-school books written by "teacher-cooks"—Miss Parloa, Mrs. Lincoln, Fannie

Farmer from Boston, and Mrs. Rorer from Philadelphia. Not limiting ourselves to these library collections, we also looked to family collections, second-hand bookstores, and community libraries for sources, which allowed us to expand the range of the book. For instance, we found recipes employing a variety of cooking styles and regional dishes, which illustrate the influence of different ethnic groups on the development of the American culinary tradition. A notable example, *What Mrs. Fisher Knows about Old Southern Cooking,* published in 1881, is the first compilation of recipes by a black American woman, Abby Fisher, a former slave from Alabama, where southern favorites such as seafood and meat croquettes, pickles, and relishes are well represented.

The popularity enjoyed by the fiction was well matched with that of the cookbooks. Cookbooks that were included in the Cairns Collection were selected on account of their narrative style and techniques: many feature characters and dialogues along with recipes, and belong to a recognizable literary genre. Conversely, and at the simplest level, references to food in fiction contribute something besides verisimilitude; they add to character development and refer to shared cultural assumptions that may no longer exist among modern readers. As such, they help furnish a valuable historical and cultural record, an account of social conditions, just as cookbooks do with their own stories. They present narrators eager to share their experiences with other women. The narratives of the novels and the cookbooks both establish among the female readership a sense of community cutting across age differences, regional conditions, and class distinctions. As powerful and pleasurable fictions, as well as books of advice and compendia of practical knowledge, cookbooks and novels happily live together.

Yvonne Schofer

Acknowledgments

This literary cookbook would not have existed without its three original compilers: Loni Hayman, Joan Jones, and Anne Tedeschi, who first conceived it as a fundraiser for the Friends of the University of Wisconsin-Madison Libraries. Together they had the vision, dedication, enthusiasm, and energy required to peruse old novels and cookbooks in the William B. Cairns Collection of American Women Writers, to look for references to food and talk about food, to search for recipes, going beyond the libraries to family collections and second-hand bookstores, and to organize their selections in the original manuscript.

We are grateful to those who were kind enough to read the manuscript and to offer perceptive and useful criticism as well as expert advice. Jerry Minnich and Lillian Clark in particular deserve our gratitude for giving of their time to enrich the project.

Special thanks go to Jennifer Stibitz for encouraging, typing, advising and taking many initiatives, and to John Tortorice for helping with the organization and preparation of the project in its early stages. I thank also Maggie Hogan, who, with her keen eye for errors and inconsistencies, improved the text in no small measure, and Janet Trembley, whose lovely design gave the book its final appearance.

This has been very much a collaborative project, and many others have encouraged and facilitated our work. We thank them all: the Board of the Friends of the University of Wisconsin-Madison Libraries, the General Library System Administration, and the staff and students of the Department of Special Collections, Memorial Library.

A Note about the Recipes

Although this is a historical cookbook, we wanted to present recipes that are interesting and intriguing enough for someone to try at home. But it is neither a facsimile, which would not be held to the home-test standard, nor a collection of new recipes, which would be. Although the editors have made some of the dishes presented here and have been pleased with the results, the recipes as a whole have not been systematically tested. Have fun—but proceed at your own risk!

All the cookbooks were written by women, with two exceptions: *Uncooked Foods and How to Use Them* is a husband/wife collaboration, and we liked *Dr. Chase's Third Last and Complete Receipt Book* so much that we decided to include its recipes on the grounds that many of them had been sent to him by women correspondents.

In our search for "food-talk" we found many more interesting recipes than we could possibly include here. We also found it necessary to update the materials to make them somewhat more approachable to modern cooks: thus the lists of ingredients have been made as uniform as possible. Still, in order to preserve the historic flavor, we chose to keep the original instructions, often literary documents in themselves, for each recipe. Occasional notes have been added to identify obscure ingredients or provide modern equivalents.

A few weight-to-volume conversions are listed below, as are modern oven settings. Amounts specified in old recipes were often approximate; the nineteenth-century purveyors of recipes simply assumed a largely sensory experience of cooking and offered few precise directions, other than combining the ingredients. It was not until the end of the century that the Boston Cooking School cookbooks decided that a more scientific approach required exact measurements. Commonly prepared dishes appeared in every cook's repertoire and recipe books assumed that directions were unnecessary. The recipes are therefore generally flexible.

Table of Oven Temperatures

Very low	250°–275°
Low	300°–325°
Moderate	350°–375°
Hot	400°–425°
Very hot	450°–475°
Extremely hot	500°–525°

(From *The Joy of Cooking,* 1997 edition)

Household Measures

Flour	1 pound equals 16 ounces or 3 1/2 cups 1 quart equals 1 1/4 pound (enough for one loaf of bread)
Sugar	1 pound equals 16 ounces or 2 1/4 cups
Butter	1 pound equals 4 sticks
	1 ounce equals 2 tablespoons
	"the size of a walnut" equals 1 ounce
Egg	1 egg equals 2 ounces

A teacup is roughly equivalent to 1 cup.

A tablespoon was a bit larger than the modern tablespoon.

You may want to compare these older recipes to similar ones found in modern cookbooks to help with determining measurements. Likewise, try experimenting with amounts to adjust the recipe to suit your personal tastes. The results will probably vary, but the cooking experience—the sense of connecting to the ways people made and ate food 150 years ago—will be well worth it.

Soups, Chowders, and Stews

*I*n the second department of meat-cookery, to wit, the slow and gradual application of heat for the softening and dissolution of its fibre and the extraction of its juices, common cooks are equally untrained. Where is the so-called cook who understands how to prepare soups and stews? These are precisely the articles in which a French kitchen excels. The soup-kettle, made with a double bottom, to prevent burning, is a permanent, ever-present institution, and the coarsest and most impracticable meats distilled through that alembic come out again in soups, jellies, or savory stews. The toughest cartilage, even the bones, being first cracked, are here made to give forth their hidden virtues, and to rise in delicate and appetizing forms.

One great law governs all these preparations: the application of heat must be gradual, steady, long protracted, never reaching the point of active boiling. Hours of quiet simmering dissolve all dissoluble parts, soften the sternest fibre, and unlock every minute cell in which Nature has stored away her treasures of nourishment. This careful and protracted application of heat and the skillful use of flavors constitute the two main points in all those nice preparations of meat for which the French have so many names— processes by which a delicacy can be imparted to the coarsest and cheapest food superior to that of the finest articles under less philosophic treatment.

French soups and stews are a study, and they would not be an unprofitable one to any person who wishes to live with comfort and even elegance on small means.

The American Woman's Home (1869)
Catharine Beecher and Harriet Beecher Stowe

"*But you look tired," [Robert] added, solicitously. "Would you like a cup of bouillon? Shall I stir you a toddy? Let me mix you a toddy with a drop of Angostura."*

She acceded to the suggestion of bouillon, which was grateful and acceptable. He went himself to the kitchen, which was a building apart from the cottages and lying to the rear of the house. And he himself brought her the golden-brown bouillon, in a dainty Sèvres cup, with a flaky cracker or two on the saucer.

The Awakening (1899)
Kate Chopin

Bouillon for Parties and Germans

2 pounds lean beef
1 quart cold water
1 small onion
1 bay leaf
1 stalk celery or 1/2 teaspoon
   celery seed
sprig parsley
salt and pepper
1 egg white and shell
1/2 cup cold water

Free the meat from all fat and gristle and chop it fine (your butcher can do this best). Put the meat in the soup kettle with the water, bay leaf, parsley, onion and celery; cover the kettle closely and place it on the back part of the range for two hours. Then place it over a good fire; skim at the first boil. Now place it over a moderate fire and simmer gently four hours. Strain, return it to the soup kettle, add salt and pepper. Beat the white of one egg with half a cup of cold water until thoroughly mixed. Wash the egg shell, mash it and add it to the white. In breaking the egg, take care to separate it so nicely that none of the yellow gets into the white— as the smallest portion of the yellow will prevent the bouillon from being perfectly clear. Now add the white, shell and water to the boiling bouillon; let it boil hard for ten minutes; then throw in one gill of cold water and boil five minutes longer; then take the kettle off the fire and strain through a flannel bag, add salt to taste and color with caramel—about half a teaspoonful to a quart. (See recipe for Caramel.)

Mrs. Rorer's Philadelphia Cook Book (1886)

Note: Germans are dancing parties featuring an elaborate reel dance resembling a cotillion, called a german, popular with all ages.

To Make Caramel, or Burned Sugar, for Coloring Broth

1 cup sugar
1 1/4 cup water
pinch salt

The appearance of broth is improved by being of a rich amber color. The most innocent coloring substance, which does not impair the flavor of the broth, is caramel, prepared as follows:

Put into a porcelain saucepan, say half a pound of sugar, and add a table-spoonful of water. Stir it constantly over the fire until it has a bright, dark-brown color, being very careful not to let is burn or blacken. Then add a tea-cupful of water and a little salt; let it boil a few moments longer; cool and strain it. Put it away in a close-corked bottle, and it is always ready for coloring soups.

Practical Cooking and Dinner Giving (1887)
Mary F. Henderson

"*B*ut I knowed what his poor, cranky system needed, an' I knowed how to get it into him, especially as he'd never tasted meat in all his life. From that time on, he [Mrs. Dodd's third husband, a "food crank"] never saw no meat on our table, nor no chickens, nor sea scavengers, nor nothin', but all day, while he was gone, I was busy with my soup pot, a-makin' condensed extracts of meat for flavourin' vegetables an' sauces an' so on.*

"He took mightily to my cookin' an' frequently said he'd never et such exquisite victuals. I'd make cream soups for him, an' in every one, there'd be over a cupful of solid meat jelly, as rich as the juice you find in the pan when you cook a first-class roast of beef. I'd stew potatoes in veal stock, and cook rice slow in water that had had a chicken boiled to rags in it. Once I put a cupful of raw beef juice in a can of tomatoes I was cookin' and he et a'most all of 'em.

"As he kep' on havin' more confidence in me, I kep' on usin' more an' more, an' a-usin' oyster liquor for flavourin' in most everything durin' the R months. Once he found nearly a bushel of clam-shells out behind the house an' wanted to know what they was an' what they was doin' there. I told him the fish man had give 'em to me for a border for my flower beds, which was true. I'd only paid for the clams—there wa'n't nothin' said about the shells—an' the juice from them clams livened up his soup an' vegetables for over a week."

"Mrs. Dodd's Third Husband," *At the Sign of the Jack O' Lantern* (1905)
Myrtle Reed

Chicken Consommé, or Stock

1 chicken
4 quarts water
1 onion
2 celery sticks
1 tablespoon salt
1/2 teaspoon pepper

Place a fowl, cut into pieces, in four quarts of cold water; let come slowly to the boiling-point; then draw it to the side of range and simmer for three hours. At the end of this time add one slice of onion, two sticks of celery, one tablespoonful of salt, one saltspoonful of pepper, and simmer one or two hours longer; strain into earthen bowl, and let cool without covering.

This stock may be cleared the same as beef stock, and served in cups for luncheon. It may also be mixed with gelatine, cleared, and used for aspic, in Russian salads, jellied chicken, etc.

The meat from the breast and second joints may be removed from the stock-pot, when tender, and reserved for timbales, croquettes, patties, etc.

If this soup is not rich enough, it can be reduced by opening the lid of the pot, after it has simmered the required time, and allowed to boil uncovered until as rich as desired.

The Century Cook Book (1896)
Mary Ronald

White Soup

1 chicken (or 1 pound veal, or
   use stock from clear or amber
   soup)
2 onions
1 cup celery
1 quart milk
1 tablespoon butter
1 tablespoon flour or cornstarch
1/2 teaspoon mace
1/2 teaspoon white pepper
(Optional: 3 eggs, lightly beaten)

Veal or chicken must be used for this soup; and the stock must always be prepared the day beforehand, having been flavored with two chopped onions and a cup of cut celery, or celery-seed and other seasoning, in the proportions already given. On the day it is to be used, heat a quart of milk; stir one tablespoonful of butter to a cream; add a heaping tablespoonful of flour or corn-starch, a saltspoonful of mace, and the same amount of white pepper. Stir into the boiling milk, and add to the soup. Let all boil a moment, and then pour into the tureen. Three eggs, beaten very light and stirred into the hot milk without boiling, make a still richer soup. The bones of cold roast chicken or turkey may be used in this way; and the broth of any meat, if perfectly clear, can serve as foundation, though veal or chicken is most delicate.

The Easiest Way in Housekeeping and Cooking
(1893)
Helen Campbell

Onion Soup

6 onions (medium size)
1 tablespoon butter
3 potatoes (medium size)
salt and pepper
1 pint water
1 pint chicken stock

An onion soup nicely made is one of the most healthful, consequently the best soups made. Take 6 medium-sized onions, sliced, and brown slightly in a suitable dish [skillet], with a tablespoonful of butter, adding 3 medium-sized potatoes, also sliced, and a little pepper and salt, and let all then cook an hour or two, putting into cold water, and simmer slowly. Add stock, 1 pt., season to taste, and serve hot, as all soups should be.

Remarks.—Onions, if peeled under water, saves the tears for other occasions, and does not leave an odor upon the hands.

> *Dr. Chase's Third Last and Complete Receipt Book* (1891)

*T*he *Judge kindly took charge of me, while "the bourgeois" superintended this important business, and with reading, sketching, and strolling about, the morning glided away. Twelve o'clock came, and still the preparations for starting were not yet completed.*

In my rambles about to seek out some of the finest of the wild flowers for a bouquet, before my husband's return, I came upon the camp fire of the soldiers. A tall, red-faced, light-haired young man in fatigue dress was attending a kettle of soup, the savoury steams of which were very attractive.

Seeing that I was observing his occupation, he politely laded out a tin cup full of the liquid and offered it to me.

I declined it, saying we should have our dinner immediately.

"They left me here to get their dinner," said he, apparently not displeased to have someone to talk to; "and I thought I might as well make some soup. Down on the German Flats, where I come from, they always like soup."

> *Wau-Bun* (1857)
> Mrs. John H. Kinzie

Thick Vegetable Soup

1 quart stock (chicken or beef)
1 quart water
1/4 cup pearl barley
1 turnip
1 carrot
6 stalks celery
2 onions
2 pounds cabbage
3 potatoes
salt and pepper

One quart of the sediment which is left from the clear stock, one quart of water, one-fourth of a cupful of pearl barley, one good-sized white turnip, one carrot, half a head of celery, two onions, about two pounds of cabbage, three potatoes, salt and pepper. Wash the barley and put it on in the quart of water, and simmer gently for two hours. Then add all the vegetables (except the potatoes), cut very fine, and the quart of stock. Boil gently for one hour and a half, then add the potatoes and the salt and pepper. Cook thirty minutes longer. When there is no stock, take two pounds of beef and two quarts of water. Cook beef, barley and water two hours, and add the vegetables as before. The meat can be served with the soup or as a separate dish.

Miss Parloa's New Cook Book (1880)

Asparagus Soup

3 pints beef stock
30 heads asparagus
1 tablespoon cream
1 tablespoon butter
1 tablespoon flour
1 cup spinach

Ingredients: Three pints of beef soup or stock, thirty heads of asparagus, a little cream, butter, flour, and a little spinach.

Cut the tops off the asparagus, about half an inch long, and boil the rest. Cut off all the tender portions, and rub them through a sieve, adding a little salt. Warm three pints of stock, add a roux made of a small piece of butter and a heaping tea-spoonful of flour; then add the asparagus pulp. Boil it slowly a quarter of an hour, stirring in two or three table-spoonfuls of cream. Color the soup with a tea-spoonful of spinach green, and, just before serving it, add the asparagus-tops, which have been separately boiled.

Practical Cooking and Dinner Giving (1887)
Mary F. Henderson

S itka, March 13, 1876
Dear Mamma,

…Did you ever eat clam chowder? I made some the other day from a recipe in the little printed book that came in one of your packages. Doctor was delighted with it, but there was rather too much of a mixture for me. When the tide is out, the beach is covered with Indians and Russians getting clams.…We all time our walks so we can go when the tide is out and we can walk on the beach. The snow has made the roads almost impossible. Doctor and I were out the other afternoon when the tide was very low and, walking down near the water edge, we found the sand just perforated with clam holes. Doctor got some sticks and we went to work for fun and soon had a mess of nice, big fellows. I was so delighted with clam digging as something to vary our life here, that we are going again in a few days with a basket. It is ever so much more fun to dig them yourself than to buy them, though you can get a whole lot for a bit.

An Army Doctor's Wife on the Frontier: Letters from Alaska and the Far West,
1874-1878 (1962)
Emily FitzGerald

A nd now I must relate the semi-tragic experience of a friend of mine apropos of chowder. Mrs. William Story was staying at a grand castle in the North of England, which was filled with distinguished guests, when one morning, as the ladies of the party were sitting together, the conversation turned on different kinds of cookery, and the hostess turning to Emelyn said, "We hear so much of your delicious American dishes, Mrs. Story, is there not some one, peculiar to your country, of which you could give the receipt to my housekeeper, and which could be made here?" Emelyn said that her good spirit deserted her, and in an evil hour she mentioned "chowder" as a fish soup belonging especially to New England. The ladies were interested at once. "Chowder," they repeated, "how charmingly Indian that sounds!" and Lady C. added, "As soon as you go to your room I will send my housekeeper to you, and we will have a New England chowder for dinner tonight and surprise the gentlemen!" And Emelyn said when she went to her room, there stood a stately dame, clothed in rich black silk, with gold watch, and chatelaine of keys hanging at her side, the mere sight of whose contemptuous English face frightened all her ideas out of her brain, and she realized what a desperate road she had entered upon. But summoning all her courage and her memory, she repeated the receipt for chowder as well as she could, trying to reassure herself by remembering how often her chowders had been praised and admired at her cottage at Nahant. The housekeeper made her a low curtesy and departed, saying with a scornful sniff, "I will do my best, Mrs. Story, but I cannot think it will be nice."

When I Lived in Salem, 1822-1866 (1937)
Caroline Howard King

Clam Chowder (The Best on Record)

2 8-ounce cans of clams, or
  2 quarts fresh clams
2 8-ounce cans of tomatoes, or
  2 quarts tomatoes
12 potatoes, peeled and diced
1 large onion, minced
8 pilot biscuits (saltine crackers)
milk, warmed
1/2 pound salt pork, minced
12 whole allspice
12 cloves
1/2 teaspoon cayenne pepper
salt
2 quarts water
(Optional: 1 tablespoon butter,
1 tablespoon browned flour)

Two quarts of long clams, chopped; two quarts of tomatoes (or one quart can); a dozen potatoes peeled, or cut into dice; one large onion, sliced thin; eight pilot biscuits; half a pound of fat salt pork, minced; twelve whole allspice, and the same of cloves; as much cayenne pepper as you can take up on the point of a knife; salt to taste; two quarts of cold water.

Fry the chopped pork crisp in a pot, take the bits out with a skimmer, and fry the minced onion until it is colored. Now put with the fat and onion the tomatoes and potatoes, the spices tied up in a bag, the water and the pepper. Cook steadily four hours. At the end of three hours and a half, add the clams and the pilot bread. This last should be broken up and soaked in warm milk. Some consider that the chowder is improved by stirring in, five minutes before serving, a tablespoonful of butter cut up in browned flour. It is delicious with, or without, this final touch.

Bills of Fare for All Seasons (1896)
Marion Harland

Fish Chowder

3 pounds fresh fish
3 large potatoes
1 large onion
1/2 pound salt pork
pepper and salt
1 pint milk
1 1/2 tablespoons butter
3 ship crackers

Cut the fish, the potatoes, and the onion into slices. Cut the pork into half-inch dice. Put the pork and the onion into a pan and sauté them a light brown. Place in alternate layers in a large saucepan first potatoes, then fish, then pork and onion; dust with salt and pepper, and continue in this order until all the materials are used. Cover the whole with boiling water and let the mixture simmer for twenty minutes. Scald a pint of milk or of cream, take it off the fire and add one and a half tablespoonfuls of butter and three broken ship crackers or the same quantity of water biscuits. Arrange the fish mixture in a mound on a dish, cover it with the softened crackers, and pour over the whole the hot milk.

The Century Cook Book (1896)
Mary Ronald

Potato Chowder

6 good-sized potatoes
1/4 pound salt pork
1 onion, sliced
1 teaspoon salt
1/2 teaspoon pepper
1 tablespoon parsley, chopped
1 pint water
1 pint milk or cream
1 tablespoon flour
1 tablespoon butter

Cut the potatoes into dice, cut the pork into small pieces, and put it with the sliced onion into a frying pan, and fry until a light brown.

Put into a kettle a layer of potatoes, then a layer of onions and pork, and sprinkle with salt, pepper, and chopped parsley. Repeat this until all the potatoes, pork, onions, and parsley are in. Pour over them the grease from the pan in which the pork and onions were fried. Add one pint of water, cover, and let simmer twenty minutes. Scald the milk in a double boiler, and add it to a roux made of the flour and butter. Add this to the pot when the potatoes are tender, and stir carefully together, so as not to break the potatoes. Taste to see if the seasoning is right. Serve very hot.

This is a good dish for luncheon, or for supper in the country.

The Century Cook Book (1896)
Mary Ronald

Oyster Soup

25 oysters (1 quart)
1 cup water
1 tablespoon butter
1 tablespoon flour
1 cup milk, scalded
salt and pepper
dash of cayenne pepper or
   paprika

Scald a quart, or twenty-five, oysters in their own liquor. As soon as they are plump, or the gills curl, remove them (oysters harden if boiled). Add to the liquor a cupful of water. Make a roux of one tablespoonful each of butter and flour, dilute it with the liquor, and when it is smooth add a cupful of scalded milk or cream. Season with pepper, salt, if necessary, and a dash of cayenne or paprika; then add the oysters, and as soon as they are heated serve at once. In oyster houses finely shredded cabbage with a French dressing is served with oyster soup, and is a good accompaniment when served for luncheon. Oysters should be carefully examined, and the liquor passed through a fine sieve before being cooked, in order to remove any pieces of shell there may be in them.

The Century Cook Book (1896)
Mary Ronald

*H*e *informed me that he would like dinner at seven, was particular about his soup. With the door in my hand, I told him we had supper at six, and it would not be convenient to have dinner an hour after that. I went downstairs all of a tremble, thinking that though I could make a first-class beef stew with dumplings I knew nothing of soups. Our boarder was not expected, and it was dreadful to think that all we really had for supper was huckleberry sweet cake and cucumbers.*

A Widower and Some Spinsters (1899)
Maria Louise Pool

When Molly had cut the steak into finger-lengths, she floured the pieces lightly, and put an iron saucepan that held about three quarts on the stove, and, when it was hot, dropped in the fat of the steak, then the meat, and left them to fry at the bottom of the saucepan.

"I should think that would burn," said Mrs. Lennox.

"No, because the meat fat is there; but it has to brown very quickly, or the meat will be hard; that is why I let the saucepan get so hot. Now I want a carrot, an onion, and a turnip—all of medium size."

"I have only small onions."

"Two of those, then."

Molly washed and then began to peel them—the turnip thick, the carrot very thin.

"What can I do?" asked Mrs. Lennox.

"You can chop that suet very fine, taking away all skin and veins."

Molly cut the vegetables into slices a quarter of an inch thick, made piles of half a dozen slices of carrot, then cut across them at even distances; it was more quickly done than the usual hit or miss way, and they looked far better; the turnip she did the same, and then she stirred the meat round, which was sending a savory odor through the house. The peeled onion she dropped into water, and then, with hands still in the water, cut it across at equal distances all the way through, then across again.

Ten Dollars Enough (1887)
Catherine Owen

Parsnip Stew

1/2 pound salt pork, sliced
1 pound beef or veal, cubed
1 1/2 quarts water
6 parsnips, sliced
6 medium potatoes, halved
1 tablespoon butter
pepper
1 tablespoon flour

Salt pork, 1/2 lb., cut in slices; beef or veal, 1 lb., in small pieces; stew in a saucepan with suitable amount of water. Scrape the parsnips, wash and cut into slices; also 1/2 dozen medium-sized potatoes, in halves. Put all into the pan or pot together, cover closely for half an hour, or till all are tender; then add a small bit of butter, and pepper pretty freely, dredge in a little flour, and a few minutes more is needed to cook the flour into a gravy, and serve hot.

Dr. Chase's Third Last and Complete Receipt Book (1891)

Mulligatawney Soup

1 chicken
3 small onions
1 tablespoon butter
1 tablespoon curry powder
salt to taste
4 cloves
juice of half a lemon
2 quarts cold water

Cut the chicken up as for a fricassee; cut the onions into slices. Put the butter in a frying-pan, add the chicken and onions, and stir until a nice brown; now add the curry powder, salt, cloves and lemon juice; mix well. Put into the soup kettle with the water, bring slowly to a boil, skim and simmer gently for two hours. Serve with boiled rice in a separate dish. Three rabbits may be used instead of the chicken, if preferred.

Mrs. Rorer's Philadelphia Cook Book (1886)

Irish Stew

2 pounds mutton or lamb
   chops, cut in small pieces
4 pounds potatoes
   (6-8 medium size)
1 onion
salt and pepper
1 tablespoon butter
1 pint water

Mutton cutlets, or chops, 2 lbs.; potatoes, 4 lbs., or enough for the family; 1 onion; pepper and salt.

DIRECTIONS—Cut the chops into small pieces, cracking the bones, if any; peel and slice the potatoes; shred, or chop the onion finely; butter the bottom of a stew pan, and place a layer of the sliced potatoes over the bottom, with a proper proportion of the onion upon them, and season each layer with salt, and a very little pepper; then a layer of the chops, etc., until all are in; then put on 1 pt. of cold water, cover the pan and simmer 2 hours, or until done. Serve hot, and keep hot as long as dinner lasts, by keeping the tureen covered.

Remarks.—Notwithstanding this is called an Irish stew, if it is done nicely it is quite good enough for an American. It is a very popular dish at hotels and boarding houses, and any kind of cold meats, not too fat, may be utilized in this way, remembering that if made of cooked meats, only about half the time will be required, enough only to cook the potatoes.

Dr. Chase's Third Last and Complete Receipt Book (1891)

Fish and Shellfish

I was invited to a very beautiful place called Weehawken; it was the prettiest place I ever saw in the woods for any amusement of the kind. When we arrived at Weehawken, we found a handsome house fitted up for the season; in front was a platform about one hundred feet square, with a railing round it and seats; outside this railing was a place erected for a full band of music. All commenced dancing the instant they arrived; some even before they got their things off. While I, with some others who did not dance, went to see the preparations for cooking the clams.

I was very much pleased, as it was something I had never seen before. First, they put on the ground thirty or forty logs of wood, with plenty of kindling; when these logs were burning, they put on a cart load of large stones; when these became red hot, they covered them with sea-weed. They then took fish of all kinds that could be baked sweet, and Irish potatoes, corn in the ear; rolled them all up in separate pieces of paper, laid them on the sea-weed; then they made another row of sea-weed, on which about three barrels of clams were put; then another covering of sea-weed; and so on, till there was a pile four or five feet high, and all was in a short time beautifully baked. In the meantime there was quite a circle of boards erected round this bed of clams, where the people stood around and received from those inside this circle bowls, butter, pepper and salt, and anything else they might require; then last came along a number of forks to eat with. Then commenced such an opening of clams, handing round of sweet potatoes and corn—just which you pleased to have—and all seemed to eat as if they were the most elegant things imaginable.

I sat aside and looked on, an amused spectator, as, though pressed by many to eat, and told how good they were, I could not eat them. There was an immense kettle of chowder, which they all seemed to enjoy very much. They all ate with such a relish as if they never had eaten anything so good before. There was a good deal of fun and merriment going on.

After they had finished their clams, they took another dance; then all retired to dress for a ball which was to be inside the house. They kept it up till eleven o'clock at night.

A Hairdresser's Experience in High Life (1859)
Eliza Potter

"*C*od-fish balls for breakfast on Sunday morning, of course," said Miss Lois, "and fried hasty-pudding. On Wednesday a boiled dinner. Pies on Tuesdays and Saturdays."*

The pins stood in straight rows on her pincushion; three times each week every room in the house was swept, and the floors as well as the furniture dusted. Beans were baked in an earthen pot on Saturday night, and sweet-cake was made on Thursday. . . . Winter or summer, through scarcity or plenty, Miss Lois never varied her established routine, thereby setting an example, she said, to the idle and shiftless.

Anne (1882)
Constance Woolson

Fish-Balls

1 pound cod fish
1 pound potatoes
1 egg
1 tablespoon butter
1/2 cup flour
salt pork
3 tablespoons shortening

Take equal quantities of chopped fish and potato, enough to nearly fill a tray of medium size. Add a beaten egg, and a table-spoonful of butter, melted. Mix and mash well with a wooden spoon. Roll the balls in flour, and fry them with salt pork and a little lard or beef fat. The whole surface of the balls should be gradually browned.

The Young Housekeeper's Friend (1859)
Mrs. Cornelius

Katy's Codfish

1 pound dried cod
1 pint milk
2 tablespoons butter
2 tablespoons flour or
cornstarch
1 egg

Soak pieces of codfish several hours in cold water, or wash thoroughly, heat in oven and pick fine, and place in skillet with cold water; boil a few minutes, pour off water and add fresh, boil again (if not very salty the second boiling is not necessary), and drain off as before; then add plenty of sweet milk, a good-sized piece of butter, and a thickening made of a little flour (or corn starch) mixed with cold milk until smooth like cream. Stir well, and just before taking from the fire drop in an egg, stir very briskly, and serve.

Buckeye Cookery (1880)
Estelle Woods Wilcox (ed.)

*L*ady Saunter's care of her husband would have been touching if it had *been less absurd. For some reason not understood by the Bentons, she imagined that Friday was a more trying day for her husband than any other. It may have been the day on which, when in England, he devoted most attention to parliamentary debates. Gus pretended to imagine that Lady Saunters belonged to a new order of religionists, similar to the Seventh-day Baptists, and that she observed Friday as a sacred day of rest. Certainly she kept it with a more than Sabbatical rigidity.*

On Friday, at breakfast, Lady Saunters watched her husband's plate with a keenness which must have been very exasperating to her victim.

"No fish," she would say to the waiter. "It is a relic of Romish superstition to eat fish on Friday. Besides, fish contains phosphorus, and is very stimulating to the brain."

Three Vassar Girls in Russia and Turkey (1889)
Elizabeth W. Champney

Salmon in a Mould

1 (8-ounce) can of preserved
    salmon or an equal amount of
    cold, left from a company dish
    of roast or boiled
4 tablespoons butter, melted but
    not hot
1/2 cup fine breadcrumbs
4 eggs, beaten light
season with pepper, salt, and
    minced parsley

Chop the fish fine, then rub it in a Wedgewood mortar, or in a bowl with the back of a silver spoon, adding the butter until it is a smooth paste. Beat the bread-crumbs into the eggs and season before working all together. Put into a buttered pudding-mould, and boil or steam for an hour.

Sauce for the Above

1 cup milk, heated to a boil and
    thickened with 1 tablespoon
    cornstarch
the liquor from the canned
    salmon, or if you have none,
    double the quantity of butter
2 tablespoons butter
1 raw egg
1 teaspoon anchovy, or
    mushroom, or tomato catsup
1 pinch mace
1 pinch cayenne

Put the egg in last and very carefully, boil one minute to cook it, and when the pudding is turned from the mould, pour over it. Cut in slices at table.

A nice supper-dish.

> *Breakfast, Luncheon and Tea* (1875)
> Marion Harland

Baked Halibut

2 halibut steaks (1 1/2 pounds)
1/2 cup cracker crumbs
salt and pepper
2 slices ham or salt pork
butter

Take 2 slices of halibut 1 inch thick; between them put cracker crumbs, pepper, salt, and fat pork chopped fine; put the same on top, using butter instead of pork. Bake in a small pan set into a larger pan of water. Bake till the crumbs are brown, basting frequently with the drippings.

A Book of Dorcas Dishes (1911)
Kate Douglas Wiggin (ed.)

Lobster Pudding

1 large lobster well boiled, or
   8-ounce can of preserved
   lobster
3 eggs
cayenne pepper and salt
1 teaspoon Worcestershire or
   Harvey's sauce
1/2 cup fine breadcrumbs
1/2 cup cream or rich milk
1/4 pound fat, salt pork, or
   corned ham, cut into very
   thin slices

Pound the meat and coral to a paste. Mix into this two eggs well beaten, the seasoning, the bread-crumbs, and one table-spoonful of cream. Stir all together until light. Line the pudding-mould with the sliced ham. Pour the mixture into this and fit on the top. Set into a pot or pan of boiling water, and boil steadily for one hour.

Sauce for Pudding

1/2 cup drawn butter
the remainder of the cream
a little chopped parsley
1 teaspoon anchovy sauce

Heat almost to boiling; stir in a beaten egg, and so soon as this begins to thicken, take from the fire.

Turn the pudding out carefully upon a hot dish, and pour the sauce over it. Cut with a sharp thin knife.

Send around lemon cut into eighths, to be squeezed over each slice, should the guests wish to do so.

Breakfast, Luncheon and Tea (1875)
Marion Harland

"So the day we got home, never knowin' what I was a-stirrin' up for myself, I turned in an' made a chicken an' oyster pie, an' it could n't be beat, not if I do say it as should n't. The crust was as soft an' flaky an' brown an' crisp at the edges as any I ever turned out, an' the inside was all chicken an' oysters well-nigh smothered in a thick, creamy yellow gravy."

At the Sign of the Jack O' Lantern (1905)
Myrtle Reed

Chicken Oyster Pie

1 pound cooked chicken
pie crust (for bottom and top)
24 raw oysters, or parboiled
salt and pepper
2 tablespoons butter

Cut the chicken in suitable pieces for fricassee, and prepare it as for that dish. Line a deep pie dish with a rich crust, and put in a layer of chicken with its gravy, and a layer of raw oysters; sprinkle the latter with salt, pepper and bits of butter. Proceed thus till the dish is full, and cover with a crust of pastry. Bake from 1/3 to 3/4 of an hour. Serve with gravy, made with equal parts of chicken gravy and the oyster juice, thickened with flour and seasoned with salt and pepper.

Dr. Chase's Third Last and Complete Receipt Book (1891)

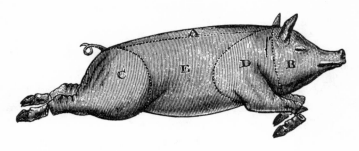

Meats

I believe in eating. The person who affects to despise it either comforts himself with private bites, or is unfitted by disease to eat at all. It does not disenchant me, as it does some, to see "a woman eat." I know that the dear creatures cannot keep up their plumpness on saw-dust, or the last "Lady's Book." I look at them as the future mothers of healthy little children; and I say mentally, Eat, my dears, and be satisfied; but be sure that you take a good walk after you have digested your food. Still there may be limits to one's tolerance even in this regard. The other morning, at a hotel breakfast, I had been contemplating with great interest a fair creature, who took her seat opposite to me, in all the freshness of a maiden's morning toilette. Smooth hair, tranquil brow, blue eyes, and a little neat white collar finishing off a very pretty morning-robe; and here you will permit me to remark that, if women did but know it, but they don't, and never will, a ball-room toilette is nothing to a neat breakfast dress. Well, my fairy read the bill of fare, while I admired the long eyelashes that swept her cheek. Straight-way she raised her pretty head, and lisped this order to the colored waiter at her elbow:

"John! Coffee, Fried Pigs' Feet, Fried Oysters, Omelette, Pork Steak."

> *Caper-Sauce: A Volume of Chit-chat about Men, Women, and Things* (1872)
> Fanny Fern

A t dinner or at lunch, if gentlemen are present, it is best to have a hot joint, a steak or some hot substantial dish of meat. Most men prefer good solid food to what they call "Kickshaws," namely, chops, sweetbreads, patties and the various dainty dishes that are favorites with women.

> *A Handbook of Hospitality for Town and Country* (1909)
> Florence Hall

I ought to tell you that some of my essays in provisioning my garrison might justly excite his contempt—they have been rather appalling to my good Mary McArthur. You know I had been used to seeing about a ten-pound sirloin of beef on Papa's table, and the first day I went into the shop I assumed an air of easy wisdom as if I had been a housekeeper all my life, and ordered just such a cut as I had seen Mamma get, with all sorts of vegetables to match, and walked home with composed dignity. When Mary saw it she threw up her hands and gave an exclamation of horror—"Miss Eva!" she said, "when will we get this all eaten up?" And verily that beef pursued us through the week most like a ghost. We had it hot, and we had it cold; we had it stewed and hashed, and made soup of it; we sliced it and we minced it, and I ate a great deal more than was good for me on purpose to "save it."

We and Our Neighbors (1875)
Harriet Beecher Stowe

Roast Beef

rib piece or loin roast,
   7–8 pounds
1/4 cup melted butter
1 cup German cooking wine
salt and pepper
1 teaspoon lemon juice

Take a rib-piece or loin-roast of seven to eight pounds. *Beat* it thoroughly all over, lay it in the roasting dish and baste it with melted butter. Put it inside the well-heated oven, and baste frequently with its own fat, which will make it brown and tender. If, when it is cooking fast, the gravy is growing too brown, turn a glass of German cooking wine into the bottom of the pan, and repeat this as often as the gravy cooks away. The roast needs about two hours time to be done, and must be brown outside but inside still a little red. Season with salt and pepper. Squeeze a little lemon juice over it, and also turn the gravy upon it, after skimming off all fat.

Buckeye Cookery (1880)
Estelle Woods Wilcox (ed.)

Roast Beef with Pudding

1 beef roast
1 pint milk
3 eggs
3 cups flour
pinch of salt

Bake exactly as directed for ordinary roast for the table; then make a Yorkshire pudding, to eat like vegetables with the roast, as follows: For every pint of milk take three eggs, three cups of flour, and a pinch of salt; stir to a smooth batter, and pour into the dripping-pan under the meat; half an hour before it is done.

Buckeye Cookery (1880)
Estelle Woods Wilcox (ed.)

Alamode Beef

2-3 pounds round of beef
3 slices dry bread
1/2 cup shortening
1 tablespoon thyme or summer
  savory
1 teaspoon nutmeg
1/2 teaspoon ground cloves
1 egg yolk
1 pint claret
allspice

Tie up a round of beef so as to keep it in shape; make a stuffing of grated bread, suet, sweet herbs, quarter of an ounce of nutmeg, a few cloves pounded, yolk of an egg. Cut holes in the beef and put in the stuffing, leaving about half the stuffing to be made into balls. Tie the beef up in a cloth, just cover it with water, let it boil an hour and a half; then turn it, and let it boil an hour and a half more; then turn out the liquor, and put some skewers across the bottom of the pot, and lay the beef upon it, to brown; turn it that it may brown on both sides. Put a pint of claret, and some allspice and cloves into the liquor, and boil some balls, made of the stuffing in it.

The American Frugal Housewife (1835)
Lydia Maria Child

Boston Brown Hash

1 pound leftover meat
1 1/2 pounds potatoes (cooked and mashed)
1 cup breadcrumbs
salt and pepper
1 tablespoon butter
1/2 cup gravy

Chop any remains of steaks, roasts or stews very fine. Grease deep pie-dishes. Put a layer of mashed potatoes (cold ones, left over, will answer) in the bottom of the dish, then a layer of meat, then a layer of stale bread crumbs; sprinkle with salt and pepper; place here and there a few bits of butter, and moisten with a half-cup of beef gravy, then another layer of potatoes. Dip a knife into milk and smooth over the top. Bake in a moderate oven about a half hour, until a nice brown. Serve hot.

Mrs. Rorer's Philadelphia Cook Book (1886)

*B**efore the fire stood a pretty good-sized kettle, and a very appetizing smell came from it to Ellen's nose. In spite of sorrow and anxiety her ride had made her hungry. It was not without pleasure that she saw her kind hostess arm herself with a deep plate and tin dipper, and carefully taking off the pot-cover so that no drops might fall on the hearth, proceed to ladle out a goodly supply of what Ellen knew was that excellent country dish called pot-pie. Excellent it is when well made, and that was Miss Janet's. The pieces of crust were white and light like new bread; the very tit-bits of the meat she culled out for Ellen; and the soup gravy poured over all would have met even Miss Fortune's wishes, from its just degree of richness and exact seasoning.*

The Wide, Wide World (1852)
Susan Warner

Mutton and Pork Stew

3 pounds mutton, lamb, veal,
    beef, or pork ribs
1/2 pound salt pork
1 onion
salt and pepper
1 tablespoon parsley, thyme, or
    summer savory
1 cup milk
2 tablespoons flour
(optional: corn)

Crust:
4 cups flour
3 tablespoons lard
2 1/2 cups of milk
1 teaspoon salt
1 teaspoon baking soda
2 teaspoons cream of tartar

Neck, or other cheap parts of mutton, 3 lbs.; salt pork, 1/2 lb.; 1 onion; salt and pepper; and parsley, thyme or summer savory, if on hand and liked. DIRECTIONS—Cut the mutton into small pieces, 3/4 or 1 inch square; the pork into small thin slices; break or slice the onion, dividing the rings if sliced. Put the mutton into a covered stew pan with cold water to cover it. Heat it gradually and stew 1 hour; then add the slices of pork, and bits of onion, the salt and pepper to taste, and continue the stewing until the meats are perfectly done, at which time, if desired, have ready some pastry, as for meat pie crust; (for 1 qt. of flour 3 table-spoonfuls of lard; 2 1/2 cups of milk; salt and soda, 1 tea-spoonful each; cream of tartar, 2 tea-spoonfuls, work quickly and don't get too stiff, or in these proportions;) roll out 1/2 an inch thick, and cut into squares, or diamonds, and put in just long enough before taking up to cook the pastry, 10 to 15 minutes will be enough; and just before taking up add the sweet herbs, if they are to be used—if put in at first their flavor will be too much evaporated. When done thicken a cup of milk with a table-spoonful or two of flour and stir in just before taking into the tureen. In place of the pastry, or dumplings, 1/2 a can of sweet corn; or in sweet corn time, the corn cut from 1/2 a dozen ears, previously cooked, may be stirred in, as an equivalent. Either plan is excellent.

Remarks.—Lamb, veal, beef, or young pork ribs, or other lean parts, make a healthful, cheap, easily digested, and a very satisfactory dinner at any season of the year.

Dr. Chase's Third Last and Complete Receipt Book (1891)

Behold us, then, on the morning of the eventful day, all stir and earnestness. The moment the professional moiety of the household left, the consultation began. I was not in the condition of Elise, whom Mrs. Gunilla relieved, at a very late hour, with a pair of chickens. My purveyor had been at his large purchases again, and I had lamb, quails, chickens, and pig. In the perplexity of choosing I turned to Hal.

"Which shall I take? for you know it is impossible to prepare more than one."

"Let it be the lamb, then, by all means. It will be more substantial as a solitary dish than chicken or quail, and will not, on an average, compel so many of your guests to cannibalism as the other four-footed animal would."

"Be quiet, Sir Impudence. I don't employ cooks to make comments on my guests. But if you think the lamb will be better than either of the other meats, let us decide upon it. How shall it be cooked?"

"You have but one way–a leg of lamb will hardly go into a three-pint saucepan. You must roast it of course; and if you have dinner at two, it must go to the fire about twelve."

"But there is a difficulty," I replied, "about roasting which my limited practice has not yet enabled me to overcome. That is to tell when the meat is done! and a small degree of over or under doing, you know, ruins the whole for nice palates."

Life in Prairie Land (1846)
Eliza Woodson Burhans Farnham

To Roast Lamb

1 leg of lamb
salt
1 cup flour

The hind quarters of lamb usually weighs from 7 to 10 pounds: this size will take about two hours to roast it. Have a brisk fire.

It must be very frequently basted while roasting, and sprinkled with a little salt, and dredged all over with flour, about half an hour before it is done.

Mrs. Hale's New Cook Book (1857)

Mint Sauce (for Roast Lamb)

4 tablespoons chopped mint
2 tablespoons sugar
1/2 cup vinegar

Put four table-spoonfuls of chopped mint, two table-spoonfuls of sugar, and a quarter of a pint of vinegar into the sauce-boat. Let it remain an hour or two before dinner, that the vinegar may become impregnated with the mint.

Practical Cooking and Dinner Giving (1887)
Mary F. Henderson

Melton Veal, or Veal Cake

3-4 pounds veal
1 1/2 pounds ham
6 eggs
1 tablespoon parsley
pepper and salt
water
1 ounce butter

Cut three or four pounds of raw veal, and half as much ham, into small pieces. If you have the remains of cooked veal or ham, add them. Boil six eggs hard, cut them in slices, and lay some of them in the bottom of a deep brown pan; shake in a little minced parsley, lay in some of the pieces of veal and ham, then add more egg, parsley, pepper, and salt; then more meat, and again parsley, pepper, and salt, till all the meat is laid in. Lastly add water enough just to cover it, and lay on about an ounce of butter shaved thin; tie over it a double paper, bake it an hour, then remove the paper, press it down with a spoon, and lay a small plate with a weight upon it, and let it remain another hour in the oven. When cold, it will cut in slices.

The Young Housekeeper's Friend (1859)
Mrs. Cornelius

Mince of Veal or Lamb

1 cup gravy, well thickened
2 tablespoons cream or rich milk
1 tablespoon butter
1/2 teaspoon mace
pepper and salt to taste, with chopped parsley
1 small onion
3 eggs, well whipped
the remains of cold roast meat, minced but not very fine

Heat the gravy to a boil, add the milk, butter, seasoning, onion, lastly the eggs, and so soon as these are stirred in, the minced meat, previously salted and peppered. Let it get smoking hot, but it must not boil. Heap in the middle of a dish, and enclose with a fence of fried potato or fried triangles of bread.

If well cooked and seasoned this is a savory entrée.

Breakfast, Luncheon and Tea (1875)
Marion Harland

Bobotee

2 tablespoons butter
1/2 small onion
2 slices of bread
1 cup milk
8 sweet almonds (1/4 cup
   blanched)
1 pint cold cooked meat,
   chopped fine
1 teaspoon curry powder
3 eggs
lemon juice

Put the butter in a frying-pan, slice into it the onion, and fry until a nice brown; add the bread and milk; take from the fire and let stand ten minutes. Blanch and chop the almonds very fine; add these, the meat, the curry, and the eggs, well beaten, to the ingredients in the frying-pan; mix all well together. Rub a deep pie-dish with butter and the juice of a lemon; put the mixture into this, and bake in a moderate oven about twenty minutes. Serve with boiled rice in a separate dish.

Mrs. Rorer's Philadelphia Cook Book (1886)

When the cutting up was all done the hams and shoulders were put in a cask by themselves and Mr. Van Brunt began to pack down the other pieces in the kits, strewing them with an abundance of salt.

"What's the use of putting all that salt with the pork, Mr. Van Brunt?" said Ellen.

"It wouldn't keep good without that; it would spoil very quick."

"Will the salt make it keep?"

"All the year round—as sweet as a nut."

"I wonder what is the reason of that," said Ellen. "Will salt make every thing keep good?"

"Every thing in the world—if it only has enough of it, and is kept dry and cool."

"Are you going to do the hams in the same way?"

"No;—they're to go in that pickle over the fire."

"In this kettle? what is in it?" said Ellen.

"You must ask Miss Fortune about that;—sugar and salt and saltpetre and molasses, and I don't know what all."

"And will this make the hams so different from the rest of the pork?"

"No; they've got to be smoked after they have laid in that for a while."

"Smoked!" said Ellen; "how?"

"Why ha'n't you been in the smoke-house? The hams has to be taken out of the pickle and hung up there; and then we make a little fire of oak chips and keep it burning night and day."

"And how long must they stay in the smoke?"

"Oh, three or four weeks or so."

"And then they are done."

"Then they are done."

"How very curious!" said Ellen. "Then it's the smoke that gives them that nice taste? I never knew smoke was good for any thing before."

The Wide, Wide World (1852)
Susan Warner

Stuffed and Baked Ham

2 ounces fine dry breadcrumbs
2 ounces brown sugar
2 tablespoons butter
1/2 teaspoon ground allspice
1/2 teaspoon ground cloves
1/2 teaspoon ground mace
salt and pepper
10-pound ham, boiled
   (to remove fat and salt)
1 egg, beaten
2 ounces more breadcrumbs
3 tablespoons sugar

After your ham is boiled, take the skin off. Take pepper, allspice, cloves and mace, well pounded; add a little bread crumbs, and a little brown sugar; mix with a little butter and water.

Gash your ham and take out plugs; fill in with the mixture. Rub the ham with an egg beaten, and grate on bread crumbs and white sugar.

Put in the oven and brown. Bake, uncovered, at 325° for 2 to 2 1/2 hours, for a long-cured ham.

To Stuff Fresh Cured Ham

Boil the ham
1/2 pound grated cracker or
   bread
1/2 pound butter
1 teaspoon allspice
1 teaspoon cloves
1 teaspoon nutmeg
1 teaspoon ginger
1 teaspoon mace
3 tablespoons sugar
celery-seed or celery
6 eggs, beaten light
1 tablespoon mustard

Mix all well together and moisten with cream, if too stiff. Whilst the ham is hot, make holes to the bone and fill with this mixture. Put in the stove to brown.

Housekeeping in Old Virginia (1879)
Marion Cabell Tyree (ed.)

Pork Royal

2 pounds fresh pork (shoulder)
6 slices bread
salt and pepper
1 onion
1/2 tablespoon sage
1/2 tablespoon thyme
1 tablespoon butter
1 cup water
4 apples, peeled and cored
2 tablespoons flour

Take a piece of shoulder of fresh pork, fill with grated bread and the crust soaked, pepper, salt, onion, sage and thyme; a bit of butter and lard. Place in a pan with some water; when about half done, place around it some large apples; when done, place your pork on a dish, with the apples round it; put flour and water on your pan, flour browned, some thyme and sage; boil, strain through a very small colander over your pork and apples.

Housekeeping in Old Virginia (1879)
Marion Cabell Tyree (ed.)

Poultry and Game

*M*rs. Peterkin thought there must be fresh sugar occasionally, as the old would have been eaten up. She felt the same about chickens. She never could understand why there were only the old, tough ones in the market, when there were certainly fresh young broods to be seen around the farm-houses every year. She supposed the market-men had begun with the old, tough fowls, and so they had to go on so. She wished they had begun the other way; and she had done her best to have the family eat up the old fowls, hoping they might, some day, get down to the young ones.

The Last of the Peterkins (1886)
Lucretia Hale

*M*amma says that she shall never go to a farm again for a "health" diet; because they fry everything, and she could n't tell what kind of meat she was eating, it was cooked so queerly; and the farmer let all the peas and corn grow so big before he picked them that they were as tough as anything, except the chickens, which were the toughest things you ever saw.

Whenever they wanted to have chicken for dinner, they would go and catch a great big hen, and take it out in front of the house, and chop its head off on an old stump, right where we could see them do it. And after the hen's head was chopped off it would run round without any head, and it took away my appetite so that I never ate chicken once while I was at the farm; and Chamomilla and Ipecacuanha cried and cried all the first day after they saw a hen beheaded. They said that the farmer was the "cruelest" man they ever heard of; and they got two umbrellas and ran up behind him when he was sitting down and cleaning some harness, and hit him so hard that he would n't let them come into the barn for a long time; and then they got his best-looking straw hat and put it down on top of some sticky fly-paper to be revenged on him. They said that they should neither of them eat any more chicken as long as they lived; and they wouldn't even take chicken-broth for about six months.

Miss Belladonna: A Child of Today (1897)
Caroline Ticknor

An Excellent Way to Cook Chickens

2 chickens
stuffing for 2 chickens
1 tablespoon butter
pinch of salt, pepper, and
    nutmeg
(optional: 1/2 cup cream)

Stuff two chickens as for boiling, with a little celery seed in the dressing; truss them nicely; place them in a four-quart in pail with a tightly fitting cover, and set the pail in a large kettle partly filled with boiling water; the water should not reach more than half the height of the pail. Cover the kettle and keep it boiling, being careful that the water does not boil away. When ready to serve, pour off the gravy, thicken it, and add butter if the chickens are not fat; season to the taste with pepper, salt, and nutmeg, if liked; a gill of cream may also be added. Lay the chickens on a platter, pour the gravy over them, and garnish with vegetable rice.

In the Kitchen (1875)
Elizabeth Miller

Fried Chicken

1 chicken, cut up
1 cup flour, plus 1 tablespoon
    for making gravy
salt and pepper
approx. 1 cup fat to cook
    chicken

Cut the chicken up, separating every joint, and wash clean. Salt and pepper it, and roll into flour well. Have your fat very hot, and drop the pieces into it, and let them cook brown. The chicken is done when the fork passes easily into it. After the chicken is all cooked, leave a little of the hot fat in the skillet; then take a tablespoonful of dry flour and brown it in the fat, stirring it around, then pour water in and stir till the gravy is as thin as soup.

What Mrs. Fisher Knows about Old Southern Cooking (1881)

Chicken Soufflé

1 tablespoon butter
1 tablespoon flour
1 cup milk
1/2 teaspoon salt
dash of pepper
1 tablespoon chopped parsley
10 drops onion juice
3 eggs, separated
1 cup minced chicken

Make a white sauce by putting the butter in a saucepan or double boiler. When melted add the flour, and cook a moment without browning. Then add slowly the milk, and stir till smooth. Season with salt, pepper, parsley, and onion juice. There should be one cupful of the sauce. Remove from the fire, and stir in the beaten yolks of three eggs; then add a cupful of chicken chopped fine. Stir the mixture over the fire a minute until the egg has a little thickened; then set aside to cool. Rub a little butter over the top, so it will not form a crust. When time to serve beat very stiff the whites of the three eggs, and stir them lightly into the cold chicken mixture. Put it into a pudding dish, and bake in hot oven for twenty minutes. Serve at once in the same dish. This is a soufflé, so the whites of the eggs must not be added until it is time for it to go into the oven, and it will fall if not served immediately after it comes from the over. This dish may be made with any kind of meat. Chicken soufflé may be baked in paper boxes, and served as an entrée.

The Century Cook Book (1896)
Mary Ronald

Chicken Pie

2 chickens
3 slices ham or pork
1 tablespoon butter
1 tablespoon flour
pie crust

Joint the chickens, which should be young and tender; boil them in just sufficient water to cover them. When nearly tender take them out of the liquor and lay them in a deep pudding-dish, lined with pie-crust. To each layer of chicken put three or four slices of pork, add a little of the liquor in which they were boiled, and a couple of ounces of butter cut into small pieces; sprinkle a little flour over the whole; cover it with nice pie-crust, and ornament the top with some of the pastry. Bake it in a quick oven one hour.

The Hearthstone; or, Life at Home (1886)
Laura C. Holloway

*W*ell, *it is a humiliating reflection, that the straightest road to a man's heart is through his palate. He is never so amiable as when he has discussed a roast turkey. Then's your time, "Esther," for "half his kingdom," in the shape of a new bonnet, cap, shawl, or dress. He's too complacent to dispute the matter. Strike while the iron is hot; petition for a trip to Niagara, Saratoga, the Mammoth Cave, the White Mountains, or to London, Rome, or Paris. Should he demur about it, the next day cook him another turkey, and pack your trunk while he is eating it.*

Shadows and Sunbeams: Being a Second Series of Fern Leaves from Fanny's Portfolio (1854)
Fanny Fern

My dinner had been intended to consist chiefly of a venison pasty, and fortunately the only dish among my store was of very large proportions, so that there was already smoking in the oven a pie of a size nearly equal to the famous Norwich pudding; thus, with some trifling additions to the bill of fare, we made out very well, and the master of the house had the satisfaction of hearing the impromptu dinner very much commended by his six guests.

Wau-Bun (1857)
Mrs. John H. Kinzie

Venison

1 haunch of venison
1/2 cup flour
1 cup beef stock
1 tablespoon butter

Roast a haunch like a loin or leg of veal, and about as long. Flour it thickly. Put some of the stock for gravies, or water in which beef has been boiled, into the pan, and baste it often. Half an hour before serving it add a tablespoonful of butter to the gravy, and baste it again and again.

If you use blazes [small cooking implements] at the table, roast it but an hour. Most persons like venison cooked simply, without spices. But if you choose to have a dressing, make it as for veal, with the addition of powdered clove.

Venison steaks are cooked like beef steaks.

The Young Housekeeper's Friend (1859)
Mrs. Cornelius

*W*e had hardly finished breakfast when our hunter, who had received the ammunition, returned, bringing with him about fifty fine ducks, which he had shot in little more than an hour. From that time until the close of our journey, our supply of these delicate birds was never wanting.

Wau-Bun (1857)
Mrs. John H. Kinzie

Wild Ducks, Roasted

1 duck
1 cup breadcrumbs
1 onion, minced
1 sour apple, peeled and diced
salt and pepper
1 teaspoon sage
1/2 teaspoon celery salt
2 slices bacon
(optional: dash of cayenne,
   1 tablespoon currant jelly)

Prepare for roasting as any other fowl. Parboil all kinds but Canvas back and Blue Winged Teal, for fifteen minutes, with an onion in the water to remove the fishy flavor, so disagreeable to many. Stuff with bread crumbs, seasoned with a minced onion, a sour apple, salt, pepper, sage and celery salt. Put them in the baker and lay a slice of bacon on each one. Bake in hot over from thirty to sixty minutes according to the age of the duck. I would suggest never stuffing Canvas back. Season with salt and pepper and roast in a hot oven thirty to forty-five minutes. Baste plentifully with butter. A dash of cayenne and a tablespoon of currant jelly added to the gravy is an improvement.

Gleaners Pride Cook Book (1897)
Compiled by the Members of the Gleaners' Society of the Congregational Church, Fort Atkinson, Wisconsin

Curried Rabbit

1 rabbit, jointed
1/2 pound fat salt pork
1 onion, sliced
parsley
salt and pepper
1 tablespoon cornstarch
1 teaspoon curry powder
1/2 cup cream
2 eggs, well-beaten

Soak the jointed rabbit half an hour in cold salt-and-water, then put into a saucepan with the pork cut into strips, the onion and parsley, and stew steadily, not fast, in enough cold water to cover all, for an hour, or until the rabbit is tender. Take out the meat and lay on a covered chafing-dish to keep warm, while you boil the gravy five minutes longer. Let it stand a few minutes for the fat to rise, skim it and strain. Return to the fire; let it almost boil, when put in the corn-starch. Stir to thickening, put in the curry-powder, the rabbit and pork, and let all stand covered, in a vessel of boiling water, fifteen minutes. Take up the meat, pile upon the chafing-dish; add to the gravy the cream and eggs, and stir one minute before pouring over the meat. All should stand, covered, in the hot-water chafing-dish about five minutes before going to table.

No arbitrary rule can be given as to the length of time it is necessary to cook game before it will be tender, since there are so many degrees of toughness in the best of that recommended by your reliable provision merchant as "just right."

Hence, my oft-reiterated clause, "or, until tender."

You can curry chicken in the same manner as rabbit.

Breakfast, Luncheon and Tea (1875)
Marion Harland

Vegetables

A traveler can not but be struck with our national plenteousness, on returning from a Continental tour, and going directly from the ship to a New-York hotel, in the bounteous season of autumn. For months habituated to neat little bits of chop or poultry, garnished with the inevitable cauliflower or potato, which seemed to be the sole possibility after the reign of green-peas was over; to sit down all at once to such a carnival! to such ripe, juicy tomatoes, raw or cooked; cucumbers in brittle slices; rich, yellow sweet-potatoes; broad lima-beans, and beans of other and various names; tempting ears of Indian-corn steaming in enormous piles; great smoking tureens of the savory succotash, an Indian gift to the table for which civilization need not blush; sliced egg-plant in delicate fritters; and marrow-squashes, of creamy pulp and sweetness; a rich variety, embarrassing to the appetite, and perplexing to the choice.

The American Woman's Home (1869)
Catharine Beecher and Harriet Beecher Stowe

There was sweet, crisp lettuce and tender radishes in scarlet coats, there were green peas, and beans, and beets, and onions, and potatoes, with dessert of wild gooseberries and plums, which latter were furnished gratis by the gracious mother in the woods nearby. Appetizing food is not the sole foundation of human happiness and progress, but it is surely one of the pillars thereof.

The Squatter Sovereign (1883)
Mary A. Humphrey

Stewed Beets with Onions

1 pound beets
1/4-1/2 pound white onions,
  sliced
salt and pepper
2 tablespoons butter
1 tablespoon flour
water or milk

Pare thinly, and slice thinly, and put with some sliced onions, 1/4 to 1/2 as much, according to the fondness of the family for onions, putting into a stew-pan with pepper, salt, and butter rubbed with a little flour; stir into hot water or milk enough to cover them well, and stew till the beets are tender. Young beets will require about an hour, old ones longer. Serve hot at dinner.

Dr. Chase's Third Last and Complete Receipt Book (1891)

Lettuce Peas

4 hearts of lettuce
2 quarts shelled green peas
2 tablespoons sugar
a few mint leaves
1 slice ham
1/4 pound butter
2 tablespoons flour
2 tablespoons water
pinch of pepper
1/2 pint cream

Having washed four lettuces and stripped off the outside leaves, take the hearts and chop them up very fine; put them into a stewpan with two quarts of freshly-shelled green peas, a few lumps of loaf sugar and a few leaves of green mint, finely minced. Add a slice of cold ham, and a quarter of a pound of butter, divided into four pieces and rolled in flour, two tablespoonfuls of water and a pinch of black pepper. Let all stew for half an hour, or longer, if the peas are not tender. Take out the ham and add half a pint of cream. Stew five minutes longer, and serve hot.

The Godey's Lady's Book Receipts (1870)
S. Annie Frost

Carrots with Curry

1 pound carrots, cut in quarters
   lengthwise
1 quart water
1/4 cup liquid retained from
   cooking carrots
1/2 cup cream
1 tablespoon butter
1/2 tablespoon flour
pinch of salt
1 teaspoon curry power

Stew young carrots and cut them in four lengthwise; to half a gill of water in which they were stewed add one gill of cream, and an ounce of butter rubbed with half a tablespoonful of flour, a little salt, and a teaspoonful of curry powder; let it simmer in a saucepan until thickened; slide in the carrots, cover for a few moments, then serve hot.

> *In the Kitchen* (1875)
> Elizabeth Miller

Stuffed Spanish Onions

6 medium red onions
1 cup cooked meat or fish
3 tablespoons bread crumbs
1 cup water or milk

Boil onions until tender, take out middles, and mix them with cooked chopped meat or fish. Put this mixture back into onion shells, with crumbs on top, and place all in baking dish with a little water or milk (if milk, add when nearly done), and bake until very tender.

> *A Book of Dorcas Dishes* (1911)
> Kate Douglas Wiggin (ed.)

O! New England, here could I shed salt tears at the thought of thy baked beans, for Gotham knows them not. Alluding to that edible, I am met with a pitying sneer, accompanied with that dread word to snobs—"provincial!" It is ever thus, my peerless, with the envy which cannot attain to the perfection it derides. For you should see, my thrifty New England, the watery, white-livered, tasteless, swimmy, sticky poultice which Gotham christens "baked beans." My soul revolts at it. It is an unfeeling, wretched mockery of the rich, brown, crispy, succulent contents of that "platter"—yes, platter—I will say it!—which erst delighted my eyes in the days when I swallowed the Catechism without a question as to its infallibility. The flavor of the beans "haunts memory still."

Ruth Hall: A Domestic Tale of the Present Time (1855)
Fanny Fern

Boston Baked Beans

3 pints dry beans
1 1/2 pounds salt pork
water
1/2 cup molasses

An excellent and favorite dish with every New England family, if carefully prepared: Get a red, earthen jar (I believe the red ones are unglazed and, therefore, preferred). It should be 14 to 16 inches deep, with a wide mouth. Get the beans at a first-class grocery, lest they should be old or poor in quality; pick, wash and soak them over night in plenty of cold water; scald them the next day with a tea-spoonful of soda; they should not boil unless they have been long stored. Drain off the water twice, at least, to remove the taste of the soda, and to each 3 pts. of beans, before soaking, allow 1 1/2 lbs. of good, sweet, salt pork—a rib piece, not too fat, is best. Let the beans cover all but the top of the pork, which must have been freshened if very salty, the rind scraped and scored; adding hot water enough to cover the beans, in which half a small cup of molasses has been dissolved. They should be put in the oven at bed-time, while there is still a moderate fire remaining. They will be ready in the morning. If the pork is not very salt, add a little salt to the water in which the beans are baked.

Dr. Chase's Third Last and Complete Receipt Book (1891)

Lentil Rolls

1/2 cup lentils
1/2 cup rice
1/2 cup chopped ham
 (or uncooked veal or chicken)
1/4 teaspoon powdered
 coriander seed
salt and cayenne pepper
12 nice vine leaves

Boil the lentils, then drain, and mix with the rice (well washed), ham, veal, or chicken, coriander seed, salt, and cayenne. Scald the vine leaves, and shake carefully, to dry. Put two tablespoonfuls of the mixture in each leaf, roll loosely, allowing room for the rice to swell, and tie with darning cotton. Lay these rolls in the bottom of a large saucepan, cover with stock; add one bay leaf, a small onion cut in slices, four cloves, and a blade of mace; cover the saucepan, and stew slowly for three-quarters of an hour. When done, take out carefully with a slice, remove the strings, and arrange the rolls neatly on a heated dish. Put one tablespoonful of butter in a frying-pan; when melted, add one tablespoonful of flour; mix until smooth; then add a half-pint of the stock in which the rolls were boiled; stir continually until it boils, add salt and pepper to taste. Take from the fire, add the well-beaten yolk of one egg and a tablespoonful of tarragon vinegar. Pour it over the rolls, and serve.

Mrs. Rorer's Philadelphia Cook Book (1886)

E ulalia had reason to thank the providing care of Kizzie, in having supplied them so liberally with home dainties, for she could taste nothing at supper but a cup of milk. Tumblers and goblets were unknown luxuries to this family of primitive habits. A large dish of bacon and greens, flanked by tremendous hoe-cakes, was the crowning glory of the table. A remnant of a cold sweet-potato pie, and some gingerbread cakes, as large as cheeses, were extra flourishes of gentility, introduced in honour of the guests. But what chiefly attracted Eulalia's admiration was the candlestick which dignified the centre of the table—a large gourd, with a tall, majestic handle, truncated to receive a dim compound of beeswax and tallow, stood upright and towering as Cleopatra's Needle, giving an occasional contemptuous sputter, and shooting upwards a long, fierce, fiery wick.

The Planter's Northern Bride (1854)
Caroline Lee Hentz

Boiled Turnip Tops à la Créole
Navets à la Créole

1/4 peck turnip greens
1 pound fresh or salt pork
1 tablespoon salt
pepper

Wash the turnip tops, and put into a kettle of boiling water with a piece of fresh or salt pork. Let them boil slowly till tender, and then season well with salt and pepper. When tender, take out and chop, but not too fine, or leave them just as they are. Drain off all water, and serve as you would boiled cabbage, piling the turnip tops around the dish, and the salt meat or pork in the center.

Again, the Creoles boil the white turnips with the greens, cutting the former portions into quarters or semi-quarters, according to the size, and chopping the greens after cooking. Eat with pepper vinegar, as you would boiled cabbage.

The Picayune Creole Cook Book (1916)
Anonymous Contributors

*T*he field was not a promising one, and Charley was not an expert digger. The dandelions were small and scattering; but he pounced upon every little root, and the pile in his basket gradually rose, until he was obliged to press it down before he could add any more. So he combined business with pleasure; sitting in the basket to rest his tired limbs and to press down the greens, for he wanted to give honest measure....

When the greens were well pressed on one side of the handle, he turned the basket round and applied pressure to the other side; and then we went to work again, digging with a hearty good will and a determination, that made up for his ignorance and want of skill.

Uncle Barney's Fortune (Little Pitchers) (1867)
Mrs. May

Wilted Dandelions

1/4 peck dandelions (use the
    first shoots, before they
    become bitter and stringy)
1 egg
1/2 cup cream
1 tablespoon butter
2 tablespoons vinegar
salt and pepper

Cut the roots from a quarter-peck of dandelions, wash the leaves through several cold waters, drain and shake until dry. Take a handful of the leaves and cut them with a sharp knife into small pieces, and so continue until you have them all cut. Beat one egg until light, add to it a half-cup of cream, and stir over the fire until it thickens; then add a piece of butter the size of a walnut, two tablespoonfuls of vinegar, salt and pepper to taste. Now put the dandelions into this, and stir over the fire until they are all wilted and tender. Serve hot.

Mrs. Rorer's Philadelphia Cook Book (1886)

Cabbage Stewed

2 small cabbages
small piece of hot red pepper or
    1/8 teaspoon red pepper
    flakes
4 tablespoons vinegar
1 tablespoon butter
1 cup meat stock

Shred two small cabbages coarser than for cold slaw; parboil them with a small piece of red pepper added to the boiling water; then pour off the water, and add three or four table-spoonfuls of vinegar, a small piece of butter, and a large-sized ladleful of stock from the stock-pot; cover the saucepan closely, and let the cabbage simmer gently for half an hour; season with a little red pepper, if it needs more, and salt.

Practical Cooking and Dinner Giving (1887)
Mary F. Henderson

Red Cabbage à La Flamande

1 red cabbage
1 tablespoon butter
1 onion
1 bay leaf
2 cloves
1 teaspoon salt
pinch of chili pepper

Take off the outer leaves of a hard head of red cabbage and cut it in quarters. Scald, drain, and chop fine. Put it into a stewing-pan with a tablespoonful of butter, one onion, one bay leaf, two cloves, a teaspoonful of salt, and a small piece of Chili pepper. Simmer slowly for one hour, stirring occasionally. Take out the bay leaf, add a tablespoonful of fresh butter, and serve.

Mrs. Rorer's Philadelphia Cook Book (1886)

Cucumbers: Boiled, Stuffed

Boiled: Peel the cucumbers, and cut them lengthwise into quarters. Boil them in salted water until tender. Make a white sauce using cream instead of milk, if convenient. Place the well-drained cucumbers in the sauce, to be heated through; then sprinkle with chopped parsley, and serve.

Stuffed: Select large cucumbers of uniform size. Cut them in two lengthwise. With a spoon remove carefully the seeds, and fill the place with a stuffing made of equal parts of minced chicken, or any meat, and soft crumbs, seasoned, and moistened with one egg and a little stock. Round it over the top, and sprinkle with crumbs. Place the pieces in a pan with enough stock to cover the pan one half inch deep. Cook in a moderate oven one hour, or until the cucumbers are tender; replenish the stock in the pan if necessary. Remove them carefully to a hot dish. Thicken the gravy in the pan with a little cornstarch, and pour it around, not over them. This dish can be served as an entrée.

The Century Cook Book (1896)
Mary Ronald

Escaloped Parsnips

3 parsnips
3 tablespoons butter
1 teaspoon salt
pepper to taste
2 tablespoons cream or milk
1/2 cup bread crumbs

Mash 1 pint of boiled parsnips. Add 2 tablespoonfuls of butter, 1 tea-spoonful of salt, a little pepper, 2 table-spoonfuls of cream or milk. Mix the ingredients. Stir on the fire until the mixture bubbles. Turn into a buttered dish, cover with crumbs, dot with butter, and brown in the oven.

Remarks. — This gives us a new way of cooking parsnips, as well as a very nice dish.

Dr. Chase's Third Last and Complete Receipt Book (1891)

Fried Egg Plant

1 fine eggplant
2 eggs
1/2 cup milk
a little salt

Flour for thin batter, and lard, or dripping, for frying. Slice and pare the egg-plant, and lay in salt-and-water one hour. Wipe perfectly dry, make a batter as directed above, dip each piece in it, and fry to a fine brown. Drain dry, and serve on hot, flat dish.

Breakfast, Luncheon and Tea (1875)
Marion Harland

*A*ny housewife can imagine the emotions of Sister Hope, when she took possession of a large, dilapidated kitchen, containing an old stove and the peculiar stores out of which food was to be evolved for her little family of eleven. Cakes of maple sugar, dried peas and beans, barley and hominy, meal of all sorts, potatoes, and dried fruit. No milk, butter, cheese, tea, or meat, appeared. Even salt was considered a useless luxury and spice entirely forbidden by these lovers of Spartan simplicity. A ten years' experience of vegetarian vagaries had been good training for this new freak, and her sense of the ludicrous supported her through many trying scenes.

Unleavened bread, porridge, and water for breakfast; bread, vegetables, and water for dinner; bread, fruit, and water for supper was the bill of fare ordained by the elders. No teapot profaned that sacred stove, no gory steak cried aloud for vengeance from her chaste gridiron; and only a brave woman's taste, time, and temper were sacrificed on that domestic altar.

Silver Pitchers (1876)
Louisa May Alcott

I explained that all I wanted readers to do was to give up meat. I eat cooked foods myself, but I adopted the raw food diet because it was the most radical vegetarian diet I could imagine, and I purposed making this test as severe as possible.

That's what I say to you, you who are reading this book. Give up meat. Just try it. You don't need to banish it from your table right at the start. Stop eating it at breakfast, then after trying that for a while, drop it from your luncheon. If you are feeling a bit better after experimenting thus for a month, try getting along without it for one week. Then be thoughtful in your selection of foods, and choose for each meal one thing that contains real nourishment. Wheat, rice, beans (and there are about twelve different varieties of beans and peas), spaghetti, vegetable soup made with olive oil as stock, barley, etc., etc.

My Walk from New York to Chicago (1912)
Mrs. David Beach

Nuts and Carrots

2 medium carrots
1/2 cup pecans
1/4 cup milk
1/2 cup cream
1 teaspoon butter
salt

Put two medium carrots and a half cup of pecan meats through a fine vegetable grinder; moisten with rich milk, set on a stove a few minutes (not long enough to cook), stirring in half cup of cream, a little butter and salt. Serve.

Uncooked Foods (1904)
Mr. and Mrs. Christian

Corn Pudding

2 dozen ears of corn
1 pint milk
1/2 pound butter
3 eggs, separated
salt and pepper

Scrape with a knife two dozen ears of green corn, cutting each row through the middle. Add one pint of milk, half a pound of butter, three eggs, the whites and yolks beaten separately, a little salt, and white pepper. Stir the yolks into the milk and corn, pour into a baking-dish, stir in the whites, and bake an hour and a half.

The Century Cook Book (1896)
Mary Ronald

Pleasant Point Corn Fritters

To 1 heaping cup of corn add:
1 egg;
1/4 cup sweet milk;
1/2 cup flour;
1 heaping teaspoon baking powder;
Add a little salt and pepper.
Fry in deep lard.

> *A Book of Dorcas Dishes* (1911)
> Kate Douglas Wiggin (ed.)

Succotash

1 pint lima beans
6 ears of corn
salt and pepper
2 tablespoons butter
(optional: 1 pound salt pork)

Take pint of shelled lima beans (green), wash, cover with hot water, let stand five minutes, pour off, place over fire in hot water, and boil fifteen minutes; have ready corn from six good-sized ears, and add to beans; boil half an hour, add salt, pepper and two table-spoons butter. Be careful in cutting down corn not to cut too deep; better not cut deep enough and then scrape; after corn is added, watch carefully to keep from scorching. Or, to cook with meat, boil one pound salt pork two hours, add beans, cook fifteen minutes, then add corn, omitting butter. Or, string beans may be used, cooking one hour before adding corn.

> *Buckeye Cookery* (1880)
> Estelle Woods Wilcox (ed.)

Winter Succotash

1 pint lima beans
1 1/2 pints corn
salt and pepper
1 tablespoon butter
1/2 tablespoon flour
(optional: 1/2 cup cream plus
   1 tablespoon flour)

Wash one pint lima beans (dried when green) and one and a half pints dried corn; put beans in kettle and cover with cold water; cover corn with cold water in a tin pan, set on top of kettle of beans so that while the latter are boiling the corn may be heating and swelling; boil beans fifteen minutes, drain off, cover with boiling water, and when tender (half an hour) add corn, cooking both together for fifteen minutes; five minutes before serving, add salt, pepper and a dressing of butter and flour rubbed together, or one-half tea-cup cream or milk thickened with one table-spoon flour.

Buckeye Cookery (1880)
Estelle Woods Wilcox (ed.)

S ez I, hunchin' him, "Do be still and less go to our old place."

"Oh, no," sez he, speakin' up to the top of his voice, "don't less leave; here is such a variety!"

"Potatoes surprise," sez he; it must be that they are mealy and cooked decent; that would be about as much of a surprise as I could have about potatoes here, to have 'em biled fit to eat; we'll have some of them, anyway.

"Philadelphia caperin'—I didn't know that Philadelphia caperin' wuz any better than Chicago a-caperin' or New York a-caperin'."

> *Samantha at the World's Fair* (1893)
> Marietta Holley

Aunt Laura's Breakfast Potatoes

1 quart boiled potatoes
2 teaspoons salt
2 tablespoons butter
1/2 pint cream

This is a dish that has for forty years been the envy of many a housekeeper. The three essentials are cream, firm boiled potatoes, and patience in cutting them. The potatoes are left from dinner; select those that are not mealy, and where that is impossible pare off the mealy surface; new potatoes, not thoroughly ripe, are particularly nice for this purpose. Take a small, sharp, thin-bladed knife, and "nip" the potatoes in bits about the size of a dime, a little thinner on the edges than in the centre; put a quart of these pieces in a stewpan, in layers with two even teaspoonfuls of salt and two ounces of butter; pour half a pint of cream over the top, cover, heat slowly, and let them stew gently for eight or ten minutes; stir as little as possible, and with a fork only, and in taking them up be very careful not to break the pieces. It requires no little time to cut the potatoes properly; it was "Aunt Laura's" evening work, and instead of being additional labor, after her day's struggle in the kitchen, it seemed a recreation, as she sat, smiling and happy, while the delicate bits fell from her knife like snow-flakes into the basin below.

> *In the Kitchen* (1875)
> Elizabeth Miller

Potatoe Balls

6 potatoes, boiled
1 egg yolk
1 egg, beaten
1 cup cracker crumbs
1/4 cup oil (if frying the balls)

Mash boiled potatoes fine, stir into them the yolk of an egg, and make them into balls; then dip them into a beaten egg, roll them in cracker crumbs, and brown them in a quick oven; or, fry them in a small quantity of nice drippings, and in that case flatten them so that they can be easily turned, and browned both sides.

The Young Housekeeper's Friend (1859)
Mrs. Cornelius

Candied Sweet Potatoes

3 medium sweet potatoes or
  yams
2 tablespoons sugar
1 tablespoon butter
(optional: 1/4 cup maple syrup)

Boil the potatoes until they are thoroughly cooked, then peel and slice them. Butter a shallow dish or tin and put in a layer of potatoes. Sprinkle over this a little sugar, then put in another layer of potatoes and another of sugar, with a few bits of butter on top. A little maple syrup added before putting into the oven makes it still better. Leave in the oven only long enough to brown.

A Book of Dorcas Dishes (1911)
Kate Douglas Wiggin (ed.)

*J*ulia was laughing too much to be wholly intelligible, but read from a scrap in her apron pocket: "Any fruit in season, cold beans or peas, minced cucumber, English walnuts, a few cubes of cold meat left from dinner, hard boiled eggs in slices, flecks of ripe tomatoes and radishes to perfect the color scheme, a dash of onion juice, dash of paprika, dash of rich cream.' I have left out the okra, the shallot, the estragon, the tarragon, the endive, the hearts of artichoke, the Hungarian peppers and the haricot beans because we had n't any;— do you think it will make any difference, Aunt Margaret?"

Mother Carey's Chickens (1911)
Kate Douglas Wiggin

Cabbage Salad

1 quart cabbage
2/3 cup sour cream
2 eggs
sugar, salt, pepper, and mustard
1/2 cup celery (or 1 tablespoon
   celery seed)
1 tablespoon vinegar

One quart of very finely-chopped cabbage, two-thirds of a cup of sour cream, two well-beaten eggs; season to taste with sugar, salt, pepper and mustard. If you have no celery to chop with your cabbage, put in a tablespoonful of celery-seed. Add a little vinegar. This is very fine, will keep well several days and is excellent for picnics.

The Hearthstone; or, Life at Home (1886)
Laura C. Holloway

Pies

*T*he making of pies *at this period assumed vast proportions that verged upon the sublime. Pies were made by forties and fifties and hundreds, and made of everything on the earth and under the earth.*

The pie is an English institution, which, planted on American soil, forthwith ran rampant and burst forth into untold variety of genera and species. Not merely the old traditional mince pie, but a thousand strictly American seedlings from that main stock, evinced the power of American housewives to adapt old institutions to new uses. Pumpkin pies, cranberry pies, huckleberry pies, cherry pies, green-currant pies, peach, pear, and plum pies, custard pies, apple pies, Marlborough-pudding pies,—pies with top crusts, and pies without,—pies adorned with all sorts of fanciful flutings and architectural strips laid across and around, and otherwise varied, attested the boundless fertility of the feminine mind, when once let loose in a given direction.

    "The Slaves of the Rolling Pin," *Oldtown Folks* (1869)
    Harriet Beecher Stowe

*P*ies *again! Always pies! One, two, three, four, this is the fifth time, within, say, ten days or a fortnight, that, to my knowledge, pies have stood in the way of better things.*

First, my hostess, Mrs. Fennel, could not leave to take a ride with me a few mornings ago, because "we are entirely out of—pies...."

"Dear me!" cried breezy Mrs. Melendy, "I know what that feeling is well enough; and 'tis a dreadful feeling! Why, I should no more dare to set out a meal's victuals without pie than I should dare to fly!"

    The Schoolmaster's Trunk (1874)
    Mrs. A. M. Diaz

Plain Pie Crust

2 1/2 cups sifted flour
1 cup shortening
pinch of salt
1 heaping teaspoon baking
powder
1/2 cup water
2 pie crusts

Two and a half cupfuls of sifted flour, one cupful of shortening, half butter and half lard, cold; a pinch of salt, a heaping teaspoonful of baking powder, sifted through the flour. Rub thoroughly the shortening into the flour. Mix together with half a teacupful of cold water, or enough to form a rather stiff dough; mix as little as possible, just enough to get it into shape to roll out; it must be handled very lightly. This rule is for two pies. Great care must be taken in adding the water. Wet only the dry flour, never stirring twice in the same place, and taking care not to add more than is needed to moisten. When you have a little pie crust left, do not throw it away; roll it thin, cut it in small squares and bake. Just before tea, put a spoonful of raspberry jelly on each square.

Bills of Fare for All Seasons (1896)
Marion Harland

Lemon Pies

1 tablespoon butter
1 1/2 cup powdered sugar
4 eggs, separated
2 lemons (grated peel and juice)
1 single pie crust

Take four eggs, one tablespoonful of butter to one and a half tea-cup of powdered sugar, rub butter and sugar together until a cream, then add the yelks of the eggs to butter and sugar, and beat until light; beat the white of the egg until perfectly lightly, and add to the other. Take two lemons, roll them with your hands, on board until soft, then grate peel of lemons and put into preparation, then squeeze juice of lemons into preparation. All articles in this preparation should be well mixed together and put into pastry, and baked immediately in a hot oven. Only one layer of pastry in bottom of pie plate.

What Mrs. Fisher Knows about Old Southern Cooking (1881)

Mock Cherry Pie

1 cup cranberries
1/2 cup raisins
1 cup sugar
1/4 teaspoon salt
1 tablespoon flour
2/3 cup cold water
1 teaspoon vanilla
2 single pie crusts

One coffee cup heaping full of cranberries cut in halves, one-half cup seedless raisins cut in small pieces; mix with raisins one cup sugar, one-quarter tea-spoon salt, one heaping table-spoon flour; add cranberries and two-thirds cup cold water, one tea-spoon vanilla. Bake in two crusts.

Capital City Cook Book (1883)
Women's Guild of Grace Church, Madison, Wisconsin

Rhubarb Pie

1 quart rhubarb
1 1/2 cup sugar
1/2 teaspoon salt
1 teaspoon grated nutmeg
1 double pie crust

Cut the large stalks off where the leaves commence; strip off the outside skin, then cut the stalks in pieces half an inch long; line a pie dish with paste rolled rather thicker than a dollar piece, put in a layer of the rhubarb nearly an inch deep; to a quart bowl of cut rhubarb, put a large teacup of sugar, strew it over with a salt-spoonful of salt, and half a nutmeg grated; cover with a rich pie crust, cut a slit in the centre, trim off the edge with a sharp knife, and bake in a quick oven, until the pie loosens from the dish. Rhubarb pies made in this way, are altogether superior to those made of the fruit stewed.

The American Lady's System of Cookery
(1860)
Mrs. T. J. Crowen

ercurius just enjoyed the pie that Mrs. Brown made, and he ate it for every meal, and he said it was so good that it made him forget how awfully he was having the hay-fever. What he liked best was squash pie with maple syrup on it; he said that was "just out of sight."

All the pie was pretty much "out of sight" whenever Mercurius got at it....

At first mamma was going to forbid us to eat pie so often, but when she found that there wasn't much else to eat, she changed her mind and ate it herself.

Miss Belladonna: A Child of Today (1897)
Caroline Ticknor

Squash Pie

4 pies:
5 pints stewed and strained
  squash
2 quarts boiling milk
1 1/2 teaspoons nutmeg
4 teaspoons salt
5 cups sugar
9 eggs
3 tablespoons Madeira
2 tablespoons rose-water
4 single pie crusts

Five pints of stewed and strained squash, two quarts of boiling milk, one and a half nutmegs, four teaspoonfuls of salt, five cupfuls of sugar, nine eggs, four table-spoonfuls of Sicily Madeira and two of rose-water. Gradually pour the boiling milk on the squash, and stir continually. Add the nutmeg, rose-water and sugar. When cold, add the eggs, well beaten; and just before the mixture is put in the plates, add the Madeira. Butter deep plates, and line with a plain paste. Fill the mixture, and bake in a moderate over for forty minutes.

Miss Parloa's New Cook Book (1880)

Sweet Potato Pie

2 pounds sweet potatoes
1 tablespoon butter
5 eggs, separated
1/2 cup milk
sugar to taste (approx. 1/4 cup)
juice of 1 orange
grated peel of 1/2 orange
1/2 teaspoon salt
1 single pie crust

Two pounds of potatoes will make two pies. Boil the potatoes soft; peel and mash fine through a cullender while hot; one tablespoonful of butter to be mashed in with the potato. Take five eggs and beat the yelks and whites separate and add one gill of milk; sweeten to taste; squeeze the juice of one orange, and grate one-half of the peel into the liquid. One half teaspoonful of salt in the potatoes. Have only one crust and that at the bottom of the plate. Bake quickly.

What Mrs. Fisher Knows about Old Southern Cooking (1881)

"My dear, it goes a long way, I find, after being brought up as you and I have, on codfish and pie. When I stop to think of all the pies I used to eat back in New England, really I feel as though I owe my digestive organs a great reparation. And those awful New England 'teas' where everything is cold, and the inevitable blueberry pie—sometimes it was blueberry cake—and when it wasn't blueberries it was thick custard pie! It seems to me that, instead of the New England babies being born with a silver spoon in their mouths, they are born with pie in their mouths."

The Russells in Chicago (1902)
Emily Wheaton

Chocolate Custard Pie

4 ounces baker's chocolate,
  melted
1 pint boiling water
6 eggs, separated
1 quart milk
1/2 cup sugar
2 teaspoons vanilla
(optional: pie crust)

One-quarter cake of Baker's chocolate, grated; one pint of boiling water, six eggs, one quart of milk, one-half cupful of white sugar, two teaspoonfuls of vanilla. Dissolve the chocolate in a very little milk, stir into the boiling water, and boil three minutes. When nearly cold, beat up with this the yolks of all the eggs and whites of three. Stir this mixture into the milk, season and pour into shells of good paste [pastry]. When the custard is "set"—but not more than half done—spread over it the whites whipped to a froth, with two tablespoonfuls of sugar. You may bake these custards without paste, in a pudding-dish or cups set in boiling water.

Bills of Fare for All Seasons (1896)
Marion Harland

"If we go at one she [the hostess] will have time to prepare tea; if we wait till two, she will be compelled to dismiss us without."

"Send a messenger then to assure her that we are coming; that will give her time."...

We repaired to our post at one o'clock; the hostess was already on the qui vive. She however sat about five minutes after our entrance, to give dignity to the reception, and then went about consummating the great event of the day—the tea table. The whole affair went on in the room where we sat, so that I shall be able to give its different stages and progress with an accuracy which, I trust, may be appreciated.

First stage—half-past one—a kettle of pumpkin is suspended over the fire for stewing, and a tea-kettle placed on the hearth, a few inches from the forestick; half past two, a patent oven is placed before the fire, filled with gingerbread, of which I will give the recipe to the next edition of the Frugal Housewife. Next, the pumpkin is taken up and prepared for baking, by sifting and mixing with eggs, milk, ginger, and molasses. I ought to have remarked that as all this took place in the month of May, the pumpkin was dried.

> *Life in Prairie Land* (1846)
> Eliza Woodson Burhans Farnham

There is nothing new at this post, only it is getting colder and colder. We had our first pumpkin pies this week. I was very much pleased with them, as I tried to make them rich and nice, but Doctor said they were pretty good, only not like his mother used to make (a remark which I have punished him for a great many times). I told him I wouldn't make them any more, but I was comforted by Colonel Perry telling me to send him a whole pie the next time I made them, and that I beat his wife at pumpkin pies.

> *An Army Doctor's Wife on the Frontier: Letters from Alaska and the Far West, 1874-1878* (1962)
> Emily FitzGerald

Pumpkin Pie

1 pint stewed pumpkin
3 tablespoons butter
1 1/2 cups sugar
2 teaspoons cinnamon
1/2 teaspoon ginger
1/2 teaspoon nutmeg
6 eggs
6 tablespoons flour
1 single pie crust

Stewed pumpkin, 1 heaping pint; 6 eggs; flour, 6 table-spoonfuls; butter, size of an egg; sugar, 1 1/2 cups; cinnamon, 2 level tea-spoonfuls; ginger, 1/2 tea-spoonful; 1/2 a grated nutmeg. DIRECTIONS—Rub the pumpkin through a colander, adding the butter, sugar and spices, and make hot, then the beaten eggs and flour; mix smoothly together, and while hot put into the dish, having a thick crust to receive it, and bake in a moderate oven.

Remarks.—This makes a thick, salvy pie, very nice. If fearful of a soggy crust, bake it before putting in the pie mixture. If a pint of milk was added, it would be more like the old-fashioned pumpkin-custard pie, softer and not quite so rich, unless an additional egg or two, with an extra cup of sugar is put in. If milk is plenty, and pumpkin scarce, take this latter plan.

Dr. Chase's Third Last and Complete Receipt Book (1891)

"*Elder Sniffles will you take some o' the pie—here is mince pie and punkin pie.*"

"*I will take a small portion of the pumpkin pie if you please, Mrs. Maguire, as I consider it highly nutritious; but as regards the mince pie, it is an article of food which I deem excessively deleterious to the constitution, inasmuch as it is composed of so great a variety of ingredients. I esteem it exceedingly difficult of digestion. Is it not so my young friend?*"

"*By no means, elder; quite the contrary—and the reason is obvious. Observe, elder—it is cut into the most minute particles; hence it naturally follows, that being, as it were completely calcined before it enters the system—it leaves so to speak, no labor to be performed by the digestive organs and it is disposed of without the slightest difficulty.*"

"*Ah, indeed! your reasoning is quite new to me—yet I confess it to be most satisfactory and lucid. In consideration of its facility of digestion I will partake also of the mince pie.*"

The Widow Bedott's Papers (1884)
Frances Miriam Berry Whitcher

Mince Meat

2 pounds beef
2 pounds beef suet
4 pounds apples
2 pounds raisins
1 pound citron
2 pounds currants
2 teaspoons ground nutmeg
1/2 tablespoon cloves
1 pound candied lemon peel
2 pounds sugar
1 tablespoon cinnamon
1/2 tablespoon mace
1 teaspoon salt
juice and rind of 2 lemons
juice and rind of 2 oranges
cider

Two pounds of beef (sticking piece best), two pounds of beef's suet, two pounds of layer raisins, two pounds of currants, picked, washed, and dried, one pound of citron, two nutmegs, grated, one-quarter ounce of cloves, one-half pound of candied lemon peel, four pounds of apples, two pounds of sugar, one-half ounce of cinnamon, one-quarter ounce of mace, one teaspoon-ful of salt, juice and rind of two oranges, juice and rind of two lemons. Cover the meat with boiling water and simmer gently until tender, then stand away until cold. Shred the suet and chop it fine. Pare, core, and chop the apples. Stone the raisins. Shred the citron. When the meat is cold, chop it fine, and mix all the dry ingredients with it; then add the juice and rinds of the lemons and oranges, mix well, and thin with good sweet cider, and it is ready for immediate use. If for future use, put over the fire in a preserving kettle, let come to a boil. Put it in fruit jars and make air-tight. This will keep for months.

Bills of Fare for All Seasons (1896)
Marion Harland

Mock Minced Pies, No. 3, with Apples

crackers, double handful
8 apples
1/2 cup butter
1 cup raisins
1/2 cup molasses
1 teaspoon cinnamon
1 teaspoon cloves
1 teaspoon allspice
1/4 teaspoon salt
cider
1 double pie crust
(optional: 1–2 tablespoons
    vinegar; sugar; 1 egg white,
    beaten)

Crackers, double handful; tart apples, medium size, 8; raisins, 1 cup; butter and molasses, each 1/2 cup; ground cinnamon, cloves, and allspice, each 1 tea-spoonful; salt, 1 salt-spoonful; sugar and cider. DIRECTIONS—Roll the crackers; pare, core and chop the apples, melt the butter, and mix all, using cider to make sufficiently moist, and if the cider is not quite tart, add 1 or 2 table-spoonfuls of vinegar, with sugar enough to give the requisite sweetness, which each must judge for himself, as tastes vary so much.

Remarks.—The apples give these pies a much greater resemblance to the real, than as formerly made without apples. If they are made with a light biscuit crust, which is made with at least 1 tea-spoonful of baking powder; then wetting the bottom crust with the beaten white of an egg before the mixture is put in, even the dyspeptic may eat them, if he can eat ordinary food. They are healthful, as well as very palatable. Give the author the one with the apples when he calls upon you.

Dr. Chase's Third Last and Complete Receipt Book (1891)

Fruit

*A*t our pleasant little tea-party last week, we had in the evening some preserved apples and cream handed round, which gave general satisfaction. I was requested by one of the younger part of the community to give the recipe, and write it in poetry, with the remark that it would be better remembered. So I have chosen a measure of considerable amplification, thinking if an exercise of memory was desired, I would make it as comprehensive as possible.

Have you any Greening apples?
If you have not, take some Pippins;
Mark! I do not say they're equal
To the Greenings, for they are not.
Pare and core them very neatly;
Mind you do not waste their substance,
Nor impair their fair proportions;
Poise the household balance nicely:
In one scale, like careful Themis,
Put those flay'd and heartless apples;
In the other strew the product
Of the graceful cane, that yieldeth
Its sweet blood for our refection;
And for every pound of apples,
Weigh three quarters of that sugar,
White, and saccharine, and luscious;
Lay it in a wide-mouth'd kettle,
Cover'd o'er with limpid water.
That same kettle of bell-metal

Set upon your kitchen furnace,
And your stand beside that furnace
Take with lynx-eyed observation;
Still with silver spoon removing
All the feculence that rises
On the eddies, and the bubbles
That within that tossing caldron,
Like a realm in revolution,
The caloric disengages.
When 'tis clarified and perfect,
Plunge your apples in the liquid;
Let is percolate, and enter
Every pore, until they're tender;
Then from the hot bath remove them,
Ere their surface decomposes,
Or their rotund form is broken.
Not in headlong haste remove them,
But with kind consideration,
Cautiously with spoon of silver;
Side by side in dishes place them,
Glass or china, as shall please you.
Cut within the fragrant sirup
Lemons from the sunny tropics;
And when this transparent fluid
With the acid mildly mingles,
Saturates, and coalesces,
Pour it o'er the waiting apples.
Serve them at dessert or tea-time—
Serve them with a smile of greeting,
And each tasteful guest will like them,
For their youth and simple freshness,
Better than the year-old sweetmeats,
Candied, and defunct in flavor.

Lucy Howard's Journal (1858)
L. H. Sigourney

 *"And I love apples very much,—red, and yellow, and speckled, and green.—What a great monster!"*

"That's a Swar; that ain't as good as most of the others;—those are Seek-no-furthers."

"Seek-no-further!" said Ellen;—"what a funny name. It ought to be a mighty good apple. I shall seek further at any rate. What is this?"

"That's as good an apple as you've got in the basket; that's a real Orson pippin; a very fine kind. I'll fetch you some up from home some day though that are better than the best of those."

> *The Wide, Wide World* (1852)
> Susan Warner

Stewed Apples

Core the fruit without paring it, and put it into a glass or stoneware jar, with a cover. Set in a pot of cold water and bring to a slow boil. Leave it at the back of the range for seven or eight hours, boiling gently all the time. Let the apples get perfectly cold before you open the jar.

Eat with plenty of sugar and cream.

Only sweet apples are cooked in this manner, and they are very good.

> *Breakfast, Luncheon and Tea* (1875)
> Marion Harland

Baked Apples with Prunes and Cinnamon

6 apples
1/2 pound prunes
1/4 teaspoon cinnamon
1/2 cup water

Take good-sized apples; core and fill with cooked prunes which have been stoned and chopped fine; dust with cinnamon; pour over it a little of the prune juice, and bake. Add a little water to pan to prevent burning.

The juice of the apple and prune together makes a most appetizing fruit dish for breakfast.

Why Be Fat? (1916)
Amelia Summerville

*W*e *have steaks often for tea, instead of cold meats. And everywhere one is asked there are canned fruits. It has made me hungry just to hear Nellie speak so appetizingly of hot sugared apples and buttered apples—they're just the thing.*

The Cooking Club of Tu-Whit Hollow (1876)
Ella Farman

Brown Betty

4 cups sweetened apple sauce
3 tablespoons butter
1 cup cracker crumbs
1 teaspoon cinnamon

Put a layer of sweetened apple sauce in a buttered dish, add a few lumps butter, then a layer of cracker crumbs sprinkled with a little cinnamon, then layer of sauce, etc., making the last layer of crumbs; bake in oven, and eat hot with cold, sweetened cream.

Buckeye Cookery (1880)
Estelle Woods Wilcox (ed.)

I cooked the peaches as you told me, and they swelled to beautiful fleshy halves and tasted quite magic. The beans we fricasseed and they made a savory cream in cooking that "Aunt Emily" liked to sip.

Letters of Emily Dickinson (1931)
Mabel Loomis Todd (ed.)

Compote of Peaches

6 ripe peaches
5 tablespoons sugar
1 cup water
(optional: 1/2 teaspoon lemon
 juice, blanched kernels of 2–3
 peach stones)

Pare half a dozen ripe peaches, and stew them very softly from 18 to 20 minutes, keeping them often turned in a light syrup, made with 5 ounces of sugar, and half a pint of water boiled together for 10 minutes. Dish the fruit; reduce the syrup by quick boiling, pour it over the peaches, and serve them hot for a second-course dish, or cold for dessert. They should be quite ripe, and will be found delicious dressed thus. A little lemon-juice may be added to the syrup, and the blanched kernels of 2 or 3 peach or apricot stones.

Note: Nectarines, without being pared, may be dressed in the same manner.

Mrs. Hale's New Cook Book (1857)

Peach Meringue

1 quart milk
2 tablespoons cornstarch
1 tablespoon butter
3 eggs, separated
1/2 cup and 3 tablespoons
  powdered sugar
peaches

Put on to boil a quart of milk, omitting half a cup with which to moisten two table-spoons of corn starch; when the milk boils, add the moistened corn starch; stir constantly till thick, then remove from the fire; add one table-spoon butter, and allow the mixture to cool; then beat in the yolks of three eggs till the mixture seems light and creamy; add half a cup of powdered sugar. Cover the bottom of a well-buttered baking-dish with two or three layers of rich, juicy peaches, pared, halved and stoned; sprinkle over three table-spoons powdered sugar; pour over them the custard carefully, and bake twenty minutes, then spread with the light-beaten whites, well sweetened, and return to the oven till a light brown. To be eaten warm with a rich sauce, or cold with sweetened cream.

Buckeye Cookery (1880)
Estelle Woods Wilcox (ed.)

Fruit Compote

5 oranges, cut fine.
4 bananas, sliced fine.
Juice of 1 lemon.
1 cup strawberries, cut fine; or substitute malaga grapes
  if strawberries are out of season.
1 cup walnuts.
Sprinkle with 6 tablespoons sugar, and 1/2 teaspoon
  cinnamon.
1/2 pint whipped cream.

A Book of Dorcas Dishes (1911)
Kate Douglas Wiggin (ed.)

The next day, and the bloom of early summer was on the plains, and its deep, blue glory on the sky, Helen thought again and again what she should do for her mother. At length she remembered that some one had said that the strawberries were ripe, and that her mother had longed exceedingly for a dish of strawberries and cream.

Helen and Arthur (1853)
Caroline Lee Hentz

Strawberries and Oranges

1 quart strawberries
1/4 cup powdered sugar
1/2 cup orange juice

Cover a quart of ripe strawberries with powdered sugar. Pour over them half a teacupful of orange juice and serve at once. This is very delicious.

> *Uncooked Foods* (1904)
> Mr. and Mrs. Christian

Strawberries and Whipped Cream

1 quart strawberries
1/2 cup powdered sugar
1/2 cup cream
2 egg whites

Select nice, ripe, sweet berries, wash thoroughly, then cap and put first a layer of berries, then powdered sugar, until the dish is filled, and cover with whipped cream; beaten together with the whites of two eggs and a spoonful of powdered sugar.

> *Uncooked Foods* (1904)
> Mr. and Mrs. Christian

Iced Currants

currants
egg whites
powdered sugar

Wash and drain dry, large bunches of ripe currants, dip into beaten whites of eggs, put on sieve so they will not touch each other, sift powdered sugar thickly over them, and put in a warm place till dry. Cherries and grapes may be prepared in the same way.

> *Buckeye Cookery* (1880)
> Estelle Woods Wilcox (ed.)

Gooseberry Fool

1 quart gooseberries
2 cups sugar
1/2 cup cream

Stew gooseberries until soft, add sugar, and press through a colander (earthen is best), then make a boiled custard, or sweeten enough rich cream (about one gill to each quart), and stir carefully into the gooseberries just before sending to table.

Buckeye Cookery (1880)
Estelle Woods Wilcox (ed.)

Stewed Rhubarb

Wash the rhubarb, and cut it into pieces about one inch long. Do not peel. To every pound of rhubarb allow one pound of sugar. Put the rhubarb into a porcelain-lined or granite kettle, cover it with the sugar, and stand it on the back part of the fire until the sugar melts; then bring it to boiling point without stirring. Then turn it carefully out to cool, and it is ready for use.

Mrs. Rorer's Philadelphia Cook Book (1886)

Puddings and Ices
Puddings

I have always been cheerful, and have had every thing to make me so; but I never imagined such a flow of spirits as come over me continually since I have begun to learn housekeeping. Like a bird, I can not restrain my song. Grandfather wished me yesterday to sing to an old friend of his. I did as well as I was able. "It is not equal," said he, "to what I hear from you up stairs when you ply the broom and duster."

I wonder any young girl should be unwilling to learn cookery. She misses a positive pleasure. The French ladies are said to be very skillful in this science, and not to consider it inconsistent with a position of elegance. Since it has so much to do with health, I wonder why it should be wholly trusted to ignorant and wasteful servants. As yet, I know but little of this accomplishment, but am anxious to learn more. To-day we had unexpectedly some company to dinner. Mamma always makes it a rule on such occasions to give a cordial welcome, to produce the best she has, and make no excuses. Yet I fancied that a shade of thought passed over her mind on the subject of dessert, for which we happened to be unprepared. It was then rather late, but, hastening to the kitchen, I asked Amy to give me a quart of milk. While it was preparing to boil, I mixed four spoonfuls of flour with some cold milk, taking care that there were no lumps, and at the full boiling-point stirred it in, with a cup of sugar, and half that quantity of butter. When all was well incorporated, I took it off, and, letting it cool, added six eggs well beaten, four drops of essence of lemon, and a cup of raisins, a quantity of which we usually keep stoned, to be ready for any emergency. The pudding was baked in a deep dish, and when it came to the table, well browned, and rising lightly up, the silent look of approving delight from my loved mother more than repaid me. Besides, I was conscious that it was not only an acceptable addition to the repast, but one that might be eaten without injury, and not like some of the rich sauces and confectioner's compounds, which cause the doctor to come at the heels of the cook.

> *Lucy Howard's Journal* (1858)
> L. H. Sigourney

*T*hat night at supper Mrs. Green ordered hasty pudding and milk for their repast, although neither had any liking for that kind of food. She said that she didn't see how they could afford anything else to eat, considering what they'd got in the shed.

A Widower and Some Spinsters (1899)
Maria Louise Pool

Hasty Pudding

1 heaping cup Indian meal
   (cornmeal)
1/2 cup flour
1 pint milk
1 quart boiling water
1 teaspoon salt
1 tablespoon butter

Wet up meal and flour with the milk and stir into the boiling water. Boil hard half an hour, stirring almost constantly from the bottom. Put in salt and butter, and simmer ten minutes longer. Turn into a deep, uncovered dish, and eat with sugar and cream, or sugar and butter with nutmeg.

Our children like it.

Breakfast, Luncheon and Tea (1875)
Marion Harland

The Saturday's baking was a great event, the brick oven being heated to receive the flour bread, the flour-and-Indian, and the rye-and-Indian bread, the traditional pot of beans, the Indian pudding, and the pies; for no further cooking was to be done until Monday. We smaller girls thought it a great privilege to be allowed to watch the oven till the roof of it should be "white-hot," so that the coals could be shoveled out.

A New England Girlhood (1889)
Lucy Larcom

A Boiled Indian Pudding

1 quart milk
1 pint cornmeal
5 tablespoons West India molasses
2 tablespoons suet, chopped fine

Scald the milk, and pour it over the meal; add the other ingredients. Put the pudding into a mold or bag, and boil four hours.

Hot maple molasses and butter are eaten with this pudding.

The Century Cook Book (1896)
Mary Ronald

oday everybody is on the lookout for the steamer. I do wish it would come, for I want some letters so much. We are going to have for dessert today that Bavarian cream you sent me the recipe for at West Point. I couldn't make such lovely things unless we had a cow. When you have to buy milk it would cost too much to use up cream by the pint, but the Bavarian cream is splendid. I made it yesterday evening and Doctor and I ate one dish full before we went to bed. Some of these days soon, after I send you some more money, I am going to get you to send me some gelatine. We have to pay 50 cents silver for the little boxes that I gave one dollar for 4 at West Point, and that was greenbacks, too. The mail will bring them safely and the postage will be very little, I know. When I send for them, you might get the storekeeper to put them up for you to save you the trouble. I never knew how much I loved jelly. Some German Jewish wine dealer here, a nice old man, who (sensible man) thought Doctor did not charge him enough for medical attendance, sent him a lot of fine brandy and old, old "London Club" sherry wine. I wish I could send you a bottle. I remember you have a fondness for sherry. I think it is horrid unless in fruit cake or jelly.

An Army Doctor's Wife on the Frontier: Letters from Alaska and the Far West, 1874-1878 (1962)
Emily FitzGerald

Bavarian Cream

3 envelopes gelatin
3 pints milk or cream
3 cups sugar
8 eggs, separated
8 teaspoons vanilla

Soak half a box gelatine in cold water till thoroughly dissolved. Then add three pints milk or cream, and put on the fire till scalding hot, stirring all the while. Then take it off and add three teacups sugar and the yolks of eight eggs (by spoonfuls) stirring all the time. Set on the fire again and let it remain till quite hot. Then take it off and add the eight beaten whites and eight teaspoonfuls vanilla. Put into moulds to cool.

Housekeeping in Old Virginia (1879)
Marion Cabell Tyree (ed.)

Jelly Custards

6 eggs
1 quart milk
1 cup sugar
2 tablespoons raspberry jelly
2 tablespoons orange jelly

Make a custard of the eggs, milk and sugar; boil gently until it thickens well. Flavor when cold; fill your custard-glasses two-thirds full and heap up with the two kinds of jelly—the red upon some, the yellow on others.

Breakfast, Luncheon and Tea (1875)
Marion Harland

As we left the shanty in the early dusk to go to Mrs. Grant's "up on the aidge of the dike," we each bore two cups of blanc-mange, arranged on respective plates. Orlando, however, was not thus burdened. He only had with him his ever present sense of his own importance, and his unlimited capacity for protective barking; thus equipped he naturally felt that he was ready to go anywhere, and he cantered on ahead with the utmost satisfaction.

I ought to have mentioned that when July Burns had brought the milk and the moss together with her order, and had given us directions for the concoction, she had neglected to tell us the quantity of moss required for the given amount of milk. Our one great fear when we came to consult our judgment in the matter was that we should not use enough moss to sufficiently thicken the milk, and we kept putting in one spray after another as the milk was heating. My friend remarked several times that we should never be forgiven if the stuff should n't "set" in the cups so as to turn out like jelly. "Whatever happens," she said, "this bumonge must jell."

In a Dike Shanty (1896)
Maria Louise Pool

Blanc-Mange (Very Fine)

4 envelopes gelatin
2 quarts milk
6 almonds
3/4 cup crushed almonds
1/2 cup sugar
1 tablespoon vanilla

Dissolve one box gelatine in two quarts milk, let stand for two hours. Boil six almonds in the milk. Strain through a sifter while this is being boiled. Pound together in a mortar, two handfuls blanched almonds and half a cupful granulated sugar. Stir into the boiled milk. Add one tablespoonful vanilla, and sweeten to your taste.

Housekeeping in Old Virginia (1879)
Marion Cabell Tyree (ed.)

"*Now say, girls,*" *began Nellie, as she led the way to the kitchen, "we aren't going to bake pies altogether to-day. We are going to have a jolly old supper, that's what we are, and we are going to cook that. It is part pies, but there are other things. For one, there will be a meringue pudding. Mother showed me, and I made one yesterday, so I can teach you myself. We must bake that first, to have it cool. Let me show you what we shall eat with it as sauce.*"

She went into the pantry and brought out a large glass pitcher of thick cream.

"O, isn't that lovely?" cried Madge Hallet.

"That is just what it is! Cream through glass is lovely! Catch my mother putting the cream in anything but glass!"

Mrs. Crane was passing through the room. "Look out for the hitches!" she murmured in her daughter's ear. Then she closed the sitting-room door.

> *The Cooking Club of Tu-Whit Hollow* (1876)
> Ella Farman

Meringue Pudding or Queen of Puddings

several slices sponge cake
1/2 pound raisins
1 quart milk
8 eggs, separated
sugar

Fill a baking dish within one and a half inch of the top with slices of sponge cake, buttered slightly on both sides, scattering between the slices, seeded raisins (about half a pound). Over this pour a custard made of a quart of milk, the yolks of eight eggs, sweetened to the taste.

As soon as it has baked a light brown, make an icing of the eight whites and put it on top. Set again in the oven to brown a little. Eat with sauce of butter and sugar.

> *Housekeeping in Old Virginia* (1879)
> Marion Cabell Tyree (ed.)

Lemon Rice Pudding

1/2 pint rice
1 quart milk
3 eggs, separated
11 tablespoons sugar
grated rind of 2 lemons
juice of 2 lemons

pinch of salt

Boil a half pint of rice in a quart of milk till very soft. Add to it while hot the yolks of three eggs, three large tablespoonfuls of sugar, the grated rind of two lemons, and a little salt. If too thick, add a little cold milk. It should be a little thicker than a boiled custard. Turn it into a pudding-dish.

Beat the whites of the eggs very stiff with eight tablespoonfuls of sugar and the juice of the two lemons, and brown the top delicately in the oven. Set on ice and eat very cold.

The Century Cook Book (1896)
Mary Ronald

Simple Bread Pudding

1 loaf of stale bread
1 pint boiling milk
2 tablespoons butter
1/4 cup sugar
1/2 teaspoon nutmeg
1/2 pound currants
4 eggs
(optional: candied orange peel)

Take the crumbs of a stale roll, pour over it one pint of boiling milk, and set it by to cool. When quite cold, beat it up very fine with two ounces of butter, sifted sugar sufficient to sweeten it, grate in half a nutmeg, and add half a pound of well washed currants. Beat up four eggs separately, and then mix them up with the rest, adding, if desired, a few strips of candied orange-peel. All the ingredients must be beaten up together for about half an hour, as the lightness of the pudding depends upon that. Tie it up in a cloth and boil for an hour. When it is dished, pour a little white wine sauce over the top.

The Godey's Lady's Book Receipts (1870)
S. Annie Frost

*H*e met there several of his associates—had a "fine time and a grand dinner"—the utmost hilarity and good feeling prevailed; and Mr. Darling entertained his wife with an account of it at every meal for several weeks.

"Hester," said he one day, as they were seated at a codfish dinner, "did you ever taste a potato pudding?"

"Potato pudding! No; I never heerd of such a thing."

"Well, I wish you could, for 'tis delicious! We had one when I dined at Colonel Philpot's."

"I wonder what you didn't have at Colonel Philpot's," said Mrs. Darling. "I declare I'm tired hearing about it."

"Well, I'll tell you one thing we didn't have—we didn't have codfish. But, that pudding—I wish you'd learn how to make it; it was superb!"

"I presume so; and I guess, if I had half a dozen servants at my heels, and a thorough-trained cook into the bargain, I could have things superb, too. But, as long as I have everything to do myself, and very little to do with, I don't see how I'm to get up things in style. I wonder you can expect me to."

"I don't expect you to, Hester. You always do things to suit my taste. But that pudding was excellent; and, being made of potatoes, I thought, of course it must be economical, and—"

"Economical! That's all you know about it. What gumps men are! I'll warrant it had forty different things in it, and less potatoes than anything else. I'm no hand to fuss up. I like plain cookery, for my part."

"So do I, as a general thing. But then, you know, it's well to have something a little better than ordinary once in a while."

"Well, if you're not satisfied with my way of doing things, you must hire a cook, or go and board out." And Mrs. Darling put on her injured look, and remained silent during the rest of the dinner.

The Widow Bedott's Papers (1884)
Frances Miriam Berry Whitcher

Potato Pudding

1 pound potatoes
1/2 pound butter
1/2 pound sugar
6 egg yolks
3 egg whites
1/2 cup cream
1/2 cup wine
1 teaspoon mace
1 teaspoon nutmeg
puff pastry

One pound of potatoes, boiled, half a pound of fresh butter, half a pound of sugar, the yelks of six eggs, and whites of three, one gill of cream, one gill of wine, one teaspoonful of mace, and one of nutmeg. Bake in puff-paste.

The Godey's Lady's Book Receipts (1870)
S. Annie Frost

"*Now, Mrs. Ferris," she said, "I am going. I have finished all you told me to do.*"

"*Finished! you have not brought down the things for the pudding?*"

"*Yes.*"

"*But you have not beaten the eggs?*"

"*Yes, and ground the spice, and the coffee, and dusted the dresser, and cleaned the celery, and taken the pin-feathers out of the ducks.*"

Live and Let Live (1837)
Catharine Maria Sedgwick

Orange Roley Poley, with Lemon Sauce

light pastry
6 oranges
sugar
2 teaspoons grated orange peel
6 egg yolks
4 egg whites
1/2 pound butter
1 pound sugar
juice and grated rind of 2
    lemons

Make a light pastry as for apple dumplings, roll in oblong sheets and lay oranges peeled, sliced, and seeded, thickly all over it; sprinkle with white sugar; scatter over all a tea-spoon or two of grated orange-peel, and roll up, folding down the edges closely to keep the syrup from running out; boil in a cloth one and one-half hours. Eat with lemon-sauce prepared as follows: Six eggs, leaving out the whites of two, half pound butter, one pound sugar, juice of two lemons and rind of both grated; place over a slow fire, stir till it thickens like honey. Very nice.

Buckeye Cookery (1880)
Estelle Woods Wilcox (ed.)

Cottage Pudding

1/4 cup butter
2/3 cup sugar
1 egg
2 1/4 cups flour
4 teaspoons baking powder
1/2 teaspoon salt
1 cup milk

Cream the butter, add sugar gradually, and egg well beaten; mix and sift flour, baking powder, and salt; add alternately with milk to first mixture; turn into buttered cake-pan; bake thirty-five minutes. Serve with Vanilla or Hard Sauce.

The Boston Cooking-School Cook Book (1909)
Fannie Farmer

Blueberry Pudding

8 slices buttered bread
1 quart blueberries
1 cup and 3 tablespoons sugar
juice of 1 lemon
3 egg whites

Line a deep pudding-dish with slices of buttered bread. Fill this with alternate layers of whortleberries or blueberries, and granulated sugar. Squeeze the juice of a lemon over the whole. Cover the top with slices of bread buttered on both sides. Place a plate over the dish, and bake for an hour and a half, setting the dish in a pan of hot water.

Take the pudding from the oven, spread over the top a meringue of white of egg beaten lightly with sugar in the proportion of a tablespoonful of sugar to one egg, and return it to the oven just long enough to lightly brown the meringue. The pudding should be eaten hot with hard wine sauce.

The Century Cook Book (1896)
Mary Ronald

Red Flummery

2 quarts cranberries
1 cup water
1 pound brown sugar
1/2 pound ground rice

Stew two quarts of cranberries in a very little water, till they are all to pieces. Then strain the juice through a linen bag, and sweeten it with a pound of brown sugar. Take out a pint of the cranberry juice, and make it into a batter, with half a pound of ground rice stirred in gradually. It must be quite smooth and free from lumps. Then put the remainder of the juice into a sauce-pan; set it on hot coals; and, while it is boiling, stir in, gradually, the rice-batter. When it has boiled till quite thick and very smooth, strain it again, and put it into moulds to congeal.

Eat with sweetened cream.

Red Flummery may be made also with raspberry juice; the raspberries mashed, and stewed without any water.

Seventy-five Receipts for Pastry, Cakes, and Sweetmeats (1839)
Miss Leslie

Prune Pudding

5 egg whites
1/2 pint sugar
1/2 teaspoon vanilla
1 dozen prunes

Whites of 5 eggs, beaten very stiff.

Add 1/2 pint granulated sugar and beat well. Stir in 1/2 teaspoon vanilla; lastly, add 1 dozen prunes, after being cooked and strained. Put in a baking-dish and set in a pan of warm water and cook 20 or 30 minutes.

The Blue Grass Cook Book (1904)
Minnie C. Fox (ed.)

Ices

*A*t present we subsist principally on ice cream, Levi having invested in a freezer which really and truly freezes in five minutes, and will freeze in four, a small quantity. And to tell you the truth, the reason I am writing to you to-night is because I am afraid to go to bed after a big plateful (flavored with strawberries freshly mashed up in it and sherry wine, a jolly mixture I assure you!).

Letters of Celia Thaxter (1895)

Strawberry Ice Cream

2 pints strawberries
1 3/4 cups sugar
2 cups milk
1 1/2 tablespoons arrowroot
3 pints thin cream (half and
   half)

Wash and hull berries, sprinkle with sugar, let stand one hour, mash, and rub through a strainer. Scald one and one-half cups milk; dilute arrowroot with remaining milk, add to hot milk, and cook ten minutes in double boiler; cool, add cream, freeze to a mush, add fruit, and finish freezing.

The Boston Cooking-School Cook Book (1909)
Fannie Farmer

Chocolate Ice-Cream

half a pound Maillard's or other
  sweetened chocolate
1/2 cup boiling water
3 quarts cream
1 1/2 pints sugar

Break the chocolate into eight or ten pieces, put it in a small saucepan with the water, and stir it over a slow fire until dissolved and smooth; add by degrees a pint of the cream, then the sugar, and when well mixed the rest of the cream, and strain it into the freezer.

In the Kitchen (1875)
Elizabeth Miller

Raspberry Ice

4 cups water
1 2/3 cups sugar
2 cups raspberry juice
2 tablespoons lemon juice

Make a syrup as for Lemon Ice [boil water and sugar for twenty minutes], cool, add raspberries mashed, and squeezed through double cheese-cloth, and lemon juice; strain and freeze.

The Boston Cooking-School Cook Book (1909)
Fannie Farmer

*T*he children were sent to bed. Some went submissively; others with shrieks and protests as they were dragged away. They had been permitted to sit up till after the ice-cream, which naturally marked the limit of human indulgence.

The ice-cream was passed around with cake—gold and silver cake arranged on platters in alternate slices; it had been made and frozen during the afternoon back of the kitchen by two black women, under the supervision of Victor. It was pronounced a great success— excellent if it had only contained a little less vanilla or a little more sugar, if it had been frozen a degree harder, and if the salt might have been kept out of portions of it. Victor was proud of his achievement, and went about recommending it and urging every one to partake of it to excess.

The Awakening (1899)
Kate Chopin

Vanilla Ice Cream

1 tablespoon flour
1 cup sugar
1/8 teaspoon salt
1 egg
2 cups scalded milk
1 quart thin cream (half and half)
2 tablespoons vanilla

Mix flour, sugar, and salt, add egg slightly beaten, and milk gradually; cook over hot water twenty minutes, stirring constantly at first; should custard have curdled appearance, it will disappear in freezing. When cool, add cream and flavoring; strain and freeze.

The Boston Cooking-School Cook Book (1909)
Fannie Farmer

Vanilla Ice Cream Croquettes

Shape Vanilla Ice Cream in individual moulds, roll in macaroon dust made by pounding and sifting dry macaroons.

The Boston Cooking-School Cook Book (1909)
Fannie Farmer

*M*rs. Harcourt was doomed to meet with a sad disappointment. As the salver with the ices made its appearance, and she was congratulating herself on the display that it made, a near-sighted gentleman came in sudden contact with the waiter's arm, and the whole contents were emptied on the floor. The beautiful Russian palace of ice, formed of the frozen juices of the lemon, the pineapple, and the orange, was demolished into fragments; and the groups of snow-white doves moulded out of Jolie's delicious ice-creams, were crushed into deformity by the fall. Old ladies expressed their regrets, and some of the young ladies and gentlemen tittered aside at the unfortunate mishap; but poor Mrs. Harcourt thought of the money that was thrown away to no purpose.

The Harcourts (1837)
Hannah Lee

Water Ices

1 pint water
strained juice of 3 oranges or
approx. 1 1/2 cups fruit juice
juice of 1 lemon

Water ices are made with the juice of the orange, lemon, raspberry, or any other sort of fruit, sweetened and mixed with water. To make orange-water ice, mix with 1 pint of water the strained juice of 3 fine oranges, and that of 1 lemon. Rub some fine sugar on the peel of the orange, to give it the flavor. Make it very sweet and freeze it. Lemon ice is made in the same manner.

Mrs. Hale's New Cook Book (1857)

Currant Ice

1 quart water
1 pound sugar
1 pint currant juice
4 egg whites, beaten

Boil one quart of water and a pound of sugar until reduced about a pint—i.e., until a pint of water has boiled away; skim it, take it off the fire, and add a pint of currant-juice; when partly frozen, stir in the beaten whites of four eggs. Mold, and freeze again. A good ice for fever patients.

Practical Cooking and Dinner Giving (1887)
Mary F. Henderson

Ginger Cream Ice

1/2 pint custard
1 tablespoon ground ginger
1/2 pint cream
dash of lemon juice
2 tablespoons preserved ginger,
 diced

Make half a pint of good custard, boiling an ounce of the best ground ginger, sweeten it, add half a pint of cream, a little lemon juice, put into it when half frozen two ounces of preserved ginger cut in small dice; go on as for former ices.

Mrs. Hale's New Cook Book (1857)

Cakes

A long table was spread in the kitchen, extending nearly the whole length of the room, and busy hands soon had it resplendent with a very tempting array of refreshments. *There were platters of cold meats, tumblers of jellies, huge plates of daintily sliced bread, both white and brown, pyramids of golden butter cut to represent pine apples, generous slices of cheese, and deep dishes of Aunt Hannah's best cucumber pickles, and the golden brown doughnuts piled high in large nappies, plates of genuine cream cookies, rich soft ginger cookies, gold cake, silver cake, jelly cake, cold water cake, fruit cake, lemon, orange, cocoanut and chocolate cakes, and last, if not least in the opinion of the good people, real old-fashioned pumpkin pie.*

Rocks and Romance (1889)
Mrs. F. Barrett Johnson

Chocolate Cake

2 cups sugar
1 cup butter
3 eggs
3 cups flour
3/4 cup sour cream or milk
1 teaspoon cream of tartar
1/2 teaspoon soda

Beat the sugar and butter together; break the eggs into it one at a time; then add the flour, then the sour cream with the soda. Bake in jelly-cake pans.

Filling: two ounces of chocolate, one cupful of sugar, three-quarters cup of sweet milk; boil half-done.

Housekeeping in Old Virginia (1879)
Marion Cabell Tyree (ed.)

Jelly Cake

For marmalade:
6 oranges
1 cup sugar

For cake:
1 cup butter
2 cups sugar
3 cups flour
6 eggs, separated
2 teaspoons granulated yeast

For icing:
4 egg whites
3 tablespoons powdered sugar
1 cup coconut

For this cake make an orange marmalade and use in the place of jelly, as it makes a more delicious cake. Following are the directions: Half a dozen oranges to a teacup of granulated sugar; peel oranges and grate them, pick out the seed and pith, add sugar to oranges and stir well and put to cook; stir while cooking; twenty minutes will cook it. It must be made a day before using it for cake. For making the cake, one teacup of butter to two of sugar, three of flour and half a dozen eggs. Beat the whites and yelks of eggs separate, very light. Cream butter and sugar together, add the yelks of eggs to creamed sugar and butter, then add the whites, and add flour and stir till light. Sift two teaspoonfuls of best yeast powder with the flour. With the above directions the cake is made. Place it in the pans and put to bake; fifteen minutes will bake it. Spread marmalade over the cake after it is baked. Icing for the cake: Take the whites of four eggs and beat them very light indeed. Add three tablespoonfuls of powdered sugar, beat sugar and eggs together light, and spread on cake while cake is warm. Take one teacup of fine grated cocoanut and sprinkle over cake while icing is soft.

What Mrs. Fisher Knows about Old Southern Cooking (1881)

"Old Election," "'Lection Day" we called it, a lost holiday now, was a general training day, and it came at our most delightful season, the last of May. Lilacs and tulips were in bloom, then; and it was a picturesque fashion of the time for little girls whose parents had no flower-gardens to go around begging a bunch of lilacs, or a tulip or two. My mother always made "'Lection cake" for us on that day. It was nothing but a kind of sweetened bread with a shine of egg-and-molasses on top; but we thought it delicious.

A New England Girlhood (1889)
Lucy Larcom

Out of one basket came a snow-white table-cloth and napkins; out of another, a chafing-dish, a loaf of home-made brown bread, and a couple of pats of delicious Darlington butter. A third basket revealed a large loaf of "Election Cake," with a thick sugary frosting; a fourth was full of crisp little jumbles, made after an old family recipe and warranted to melt in the mouth. There was a pile of thin, beautifully cut sandwiches; plenty of light-buttered rolls; and a cold fowl, ready carved into portions.

A Little Country Girl (1885)
Susan Woolsey Coolidge

Election Cake

3 1/2 pounds sifted flour
2 1/2 cups strong fresh yeast
2 tablespoons molasses
1/2 cup warm water
2 pounds fresh butter
2 pounds powdered sugar
1 tablespoon cinnamon
1 teaspoon mace
2 teaspoons nutmeg
1/2 pint rich milk
14 eggs

Sift into a pan one pound of flour; and mix, in a second pan, the yeast, molasses, and the water which must be warm, but not too hot. Then stir in, gradually, the pound of flour: cover it, and set it to rise; it should be light in three hours. This is setting a sponge, as the bakers call it. While it is rising, prepare the spice and the other ingredients, among which must be two pounds and a half additional of sifted flour. Stir the butter and sugar together till quite light; and gradually the spice and the milk, and beat fourteen eggs till very smooth and thick. Then stir them gradually into the mixture, alternately with the flour. Lastly, (if it is perfectly light) mix in the sponge. Then put it immediately into the buttered tin pans, and bake it in a moderate oven. It should be eaten fresh, as no sweet cake made with yeast is so good the second day as the first. If it is probable that the whole will not come into use on the day it is baked, mix only half the above quantity.

Seventy-five Receipts for Pastry, Cakes, and Sweetmeats (1839)
Miss Leslie

Cocoanut Cake

10 egg whites
1 cup butter
3 cups sugar
3 1/2 cups flour
1 cup sweet milk
1 teaspoon soda
2 teaspoons cream of tartar
essence of lemon

Icing:
2 egg whites, unbeaten
1 1/2 cups sugar
1/4 teaspoon cream of tartar
1/2 cup fresh coconut, grated
   (reserve a little for
   decoration)

Beat the eggs very light. Cream the butter, then mix the ingredients gradually. Sift the cream of tartar with the flour, and dissolve the soda in the milk, and add to the cake last. Bake in pans; an inch thick when baked, and spread with icing [made by thoroughly blending egg whites, sugar, and cream of tartar; beat mixture for seven minutes on top of double boiler], having grated cocoanut stirred in; pile one on another, allowing a little time for drying off. In making the icing, reserve some plain for the outside of the cake. Finish off by sprinkling on the prepared cocoanut.

Housekeeping in Old Virginia (1879)
Marion Cabell Tyree (ed.)

e could not afford great entertainments, so we resolved to make a new departure. Now, in a New England country-town, the chief end of woman is cake. To make five, seven, and even ten kinds of cake is considered her duty and calling, and a tea or supper-table must offer besides, cold meats, jellies, preserved fruits, hot biscuit, hot oysters, pickles, dried beef, tea, coffee, cream; the time would fail me to recount even what I have seen. This we could not do; cake is expensive, and I don't know how to make any but sponge-cake. . . . So we boldly resolved to ask people for the evening, and give them nothing but ice-cream, lemonade, and sponge-cake.

Root-Bound and Other Sketches (1885)
Rose Terry Cooke

Sponge Cake

6 eggs, separated
1 cup sugar
1 tablespoon lemon juice
grated rind of 1/2 lemon
1 cup flour
1/4 teaspoon salt

Beat yolks until thick and lemon-colored, add sugar gradually, and continue beating, using Dover egg-beater. Add lemon juice, rind, and whites of eggs beaten until stiff and dry. When whites are partially mixed with yolks, remove beater, and carefully cut and fold in flour mixed and sifted with salt. Bake one hour in a slow oven, in an angel cake pan or deep narrow pan.

Genuine sponge cake contains no rising properties, but is made light by the quantity of air beaten into both yolks and whites of eggs, and the expansion of that air in baking. It requires a slow oven. All so-called sponge cakes which have the addition of soda and cream of tartar or baking powder require same oven temperature as butter cakes. When failures are made in Sunshine and Angel Cake, they are usually traced to baking in too slow an oven, and removing from oven before thoroughly cooked.

The Boston Cooking-School Cook Book (1909)
Fannie Farmer

"Gen. Robert Lee" Cake

10 eggs
1 pound sugar
1/2 pound flour
rind and juice of 1 orange or,
   rind of 1 lemon and juice of
   1/2 lemon

Make exactly like sponge cake, and bake in jelly-cake tins. Then take the whites of two eggs beat to a froth, and add one pound sugar, the grated rind and juice of one orange, or juice of half a lemon. Spread it on the cakes before they are perfectly cold, and place one layer on another. This quantity makes two cakes.

Housekeeping in Old Virginia (1879)
Marion Cabell Tyree (ed.)

Sunshine Cake

11 eggs (11 whites and 6 yolks)
1 1/2 cups sugar
1 cup flour
1 teaspoon cream of tartar
1 teaspoon orange extract

This is made almost exactly like angel cake. Have the whites of eleven eggs and yolks of six, one and a half cupfuls of granulated sugar, measured after one sifting; one cupful of flour, measured after sifting; one teaspoonful of cream of tartar and one of orange extract. Beat the whites to a stiff froth, and gradually beat in the sugar. Beat the yolks in a similar manner, and add them to the whites and sugar and the flavor. Finally, stir in the flour. Mix quickly and well. Bake for fifty minutes in a slow oven, using a pan like that for angel cake.

Miss Parloa's New Cook Book (1880)

Plain Icing

2 egg whites
1/2 pound powdered sugar
1 teaspoon lemon juice

Place the eggs in a refrigerator or some very cold place one hour before using. Break them carefully and beat the whites until frothy, then sift the sugar in gradually, beating all the while; add the lemon juice, and continue the beating until the icing is fine and white, and stiff enough to stand alone. Keep in a cool place until wanted. Spread with a knife dipped in ice-water. If ornaments are used, they must be placed on the cake while the ice is still moist. This may be varied by adding different flavorings, such a strawberry, pineapple, rose, vanilla, etc.

Strawberry icing should always be colored with a few drops of cochineal.

Mrs. Rorer's Philadelphia Cook Book (1886)

The feast was a noble feast, as has already been said. There was an elegant ingenuity displayed in the form of pies which delighted my heart. Once acknowledge that an American pie is far to be preferred to its humble ancestor, the English tart, and it is joyful to be reassured at a Bowden reunion that invention has not yet failed. Beside a delightful variety of material, the decorations went beyond all my former experience; dates and names were wrought in lines of pastry and frosting on the tops. There was even more elaborate reading matter on an excellent early-apple pie which we began to share and eat, precept upon precept. Mrs. Todd helped me generously to the whole word Bowden, *and consumed* Reunion *herself, save an undecipherable fragment; but the most renowned essay in cookery on the tables was a model of the old Bowden house made of durable gingerbread, with all the windows and doors in the right places, and sprigs of genuine lilac set at the front. It must have been baked in sections, in one of the last of the great brick ovens, and fastened together on the morning of the day. There was a general sigh when this fell into ruin at the feast's end, and it was shared by a great part of the assembly, not without seriousness, and as if it were a pledge and token of loyalty. I met the maker of the gingerbread house, which had called up lively remembrances of a childish story. She had the gleaming eye of an enthusiast and a look of high ideals.*

The Country of the Pointed Firs (1897)
Sarah Orne Jewett

Lafayette Gingerbread

1/2 pound brown sugar

1/2 pound fresh butter

5 eggs

1 pint molasses

4 tablespoons ginger, powdered and sifted

2 large cinnamon sticks, powdered and sifted

3 dozen grains allspice, powdered and sifted

3 dozen cloves, powdered and sifted

1 1/2 pounds flour

a little pearl-ash or sal aeratus (1/2 teaspoon baking powder)

juice and grated peel of 2 large lemons

Stir the butter and sugar to a cream. Beat the eggs very well. Pour the molasses, at once, into the butter and sugar. Add the ginger and other spice, and stir all well together.

Put in the egg and flour alternately [adding baking powder a little at a time], stirring all the time. Stir the whole very hard, and put in the lemon at the last. When the whole is mixed, stir it till very light.

Butter an earthen pan, or a thick tin or iron one, and put the gingerbread into it. Bake it in a moderate oven, an hour or more, according to its thickness. Take care that it does not burn.

> *Seventy-five Receipts for Pastry, Cakes, and Sweetmeats* (1839)
> Miss Leslie

O'Leary's Gingerbread

7 ounces butter

7 ounces sugar

3/4 cup molasses

1 tablespoon ginger

3/4 cup thick, sour milk

3 eggs, well-beaten

3/4 pound flour

1 teaspoon baking soda, dissolved in 1 tablespoon boiling water

Soften the butter and beat it with the sugar until light, stir in gradually the molasses and ginger, then the milk and the well-beaten eggs and half of the sifted flour, then the soda and the rest of the flour.

This is very nice baked in round gem-pans, particularly if it is to be eaten hot.

> *In the Kitchen* (1875)
> Elizabeth Miller

*T**he number of these large fruit-cakes would have puzzled a Northerner, who might have fancied that nothing but a nuptial festival, and the necessity for filling white boxes according to the list of the guests, could have required such pounds and pounds of frosted unwholesomeness; but it is a peculiarity of South Carolina housekeepers of a primitive date that no provision is so important as these cakes.*

Lily: A Novel (1855)
Sue Bowen

Rich Fruit Cake

1 pound fresh butter, cut up
   in 1 pound powdered sugar
12 eggs
4 cups flour, sifted
3 pounds bloom raisins
1 1/2 pounds Zante currants
3/4 pound sliced citron
1 tablespoon mace
1 tablespoon cinnamon
2 nutmegs
1 large wineglass Madeira wine
1 large wineglass French brandy
   mixed with the spices

Beat the butter and sugar together—eggs separately. Flour the fruit well, and add the flour and other ingredients, putting the fruit in last. Bake in straight side mould, as it turns out easier. One pound of blanched almonds will improve this cake. Bake until thoroughly done, then ice while warm.

Housekeeping in Old Virginia (1879)
Marion Cabell Tyree (ed.)

*I*n the buttery stood a goodly row of cakes little and big, loaves whose icings shone like snow-crust on a sunny day, little cakes with plums and little cakes without plums; all sorts of cakes. On the swinging shelf of the cellar were moulds of jelly clear and firm. In the woodhouse stood three freezers of ice-cream, "packed" and ready to turn out. Elsewhere were dishes of scalloped oysters ready for the oven, each with its little edging of crimped crackers, platters of chicken-salad, forms of blanc-mange, bowls of yellow custard topped with raspberry-and-egg like sunset-tinted avalanches, all that goes to the delectation of a country party ... sponge cakes, pound cakes, fruit cakes, "one, two, three, four," jelly, nut and other cakes.

Two Girls (1900)
Susan Woolsey Coolidge

Very Delicate Pound Cake

3/4 pound butter
2 1/4 cups white sugar
9 egg yolks
12 egg whites
3 1/2 cups flour
lemon extract

Cream the butter; add part of the sugar and yolks, and beat well; then gradually add the whites, and flour and balance of yolks. Beat well, flavor with extract of lemon, and bake in a moderate oven.

Housekeeping in Old Virginia (1879)
Marion Cabell Tyree (ed.)

Hickory-Nut Cake

1/2 cup butter
1 1/2 cups sugar
3/4 cup water
2 cups flour
4 egg whites
1 cup hickory-nut kernels
1 teaspoon baking powder

Beat the butter and sugar to a cream, then add the water and flour, stir until smooth; add half the well-beaten whites, then the nuts, then the remainder of the whites and the baking-powder. Pour into square, flat pans lined with buttered paper to the depth of three inches, and bake in a moderate oven for forty-five minutes.

Mrs. Rorer's Philadelphia Cook Book (1886)

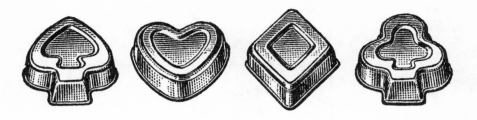

Cookies and Candy

*F*or many comforts in the household affairs of the little cabin, we were indebted to those who had preceded us. Sidney had taken the title of Mrs. the preceding year, and the festivities of the occasion had been superintended by a family of "York girls," as she designated them. During their progress she had been initiated into the mysteries of pound-cake, jumbles, and apple-tarts. And these now constituted the principal delicacies with which she tempted our appetites. It is needless to say that having only an imperfect knowledge of the rule by which they were compounded, she was not always successful in her attempts.

Life in Prairie Land (1846)
Eliza Woodson Burhans Farnham

Jumbles

1 1/2 cups sugar
2 eggs
1/2 cup butter
1/2 cup milk
1 teaspoon soda
2 teaspoons cream of tartar
lemon to taste
coconut

Mix as soft as can be handled; cut with small cutter, and sprinkle top with cocoanut.

A Book of Dorcas Dishes (1911)
Kate Douglas Wiggin (ed.)

Oatmeal Cookies

1 egg
1/4 cup sugar
1/4 cup thin cream (half and half)
1/4 cup milk
1/2 cup fine oatmeal
2 cups flour
2 teaspoons baking powder
1 teaspoon salt

Beat egg until light, add sugar, cream, and milk; then add oatmeal, flour, baking powder, and salt, mixed and sifted. Toss on a floured board, roll, cut in shape, and bake in a moderate oven.

The Boston Cooking-School Cook Book (1909)
Fannie Farmer

This holiday and all others included a constant and savory procession of cakes, from crisp, round, clove-spiced ginger ones, and thick, sugar-topped loaves, fat and black with raisins, to the flat sheets baked in shallow pans, and concocted from a recipe which my grandmother had brought with her from the German country town where she had been born. This incomparable creation of dead and gone Saxon cooks consisted of two layers, the bottom one of sweetened dough, the other a mixture of cornmeal, butter, sugar, cinnamon and handfuls of currants. You took a mouthful, and wished for nothing better in this world. In comparison to this a sack of gold was but puny dross. You forgave your enemies; you meditated giving of your goods to the poor. It was indigestible to the last degree; it had the faculty—at the first touch of lips—of crumbling into small bits and dropping down to the floor.

A Victorian Village (1929)
Lizette Woodworth Reese

Ginger Snaps

1 cup molasses
1/2 cup shortening
1 1/2 cups sugar
3 1/4 cups flour
1/2 teaspoon soda
1 tablespoon ginger
1 1/2 teaspoons salt

Heat molasses to boiling point and pour over shortening. Add dry ingredients mixed and sifted. Chill thoroughly. Toss one-fourth of mixture on a floured board and roll as thinly as possible; shape with a small round cutter, first dipped in flour. Place near together on a buttered sheet and bake in a moderate oven. Gather up the trimmings and roll with another portion of dough. During rolling, the bowl containing mixture should be kept in a cool place, or it will be necessary to add more flour to dough, which makes cookies hard rather than crisp and short.

The Boston Cooking-School Cook Book (1909)
Fannie Farmer

Boston Cookies

1 cup butter

1 1/2 cups sugar

3 eggs

1 teaspoon soda

1 1/2 tablespoons hot water

3 1/4 cups flour

1/2 teaspoon salt

1 teaspoon cinnamon

1 cup chopped nut meat,
  hickory or English walnut

1/2 cup currants

1/2 cup raisins, seeded and
  chopped

Cream the butter, add sugar gradually, and eggs well beaten. Add soda dissolved in hot water, and one-half the flour mixed and sifted with salt and cinnamon; then add nut meat, fruit, and remaining flour. Drop by spoonfuls one inch apart on a buttered sheet, and bake in a moderate oven.

The Boston Cooking-School Cook Book (1909)
Fannie Farmer

Lunch

"*S ister Jerusha, it really does wear upon me to see those dear boys eat such bad pies and stuff day after day when they ought to have good wholesome things for lunch. I actually ache to go and give each one of 'em a nice piece of bread-and-butter or one of our big cookies," said kind Miss Mehitable Plummer, taking up her knitting after a long look at the swarm of boys pouring out of the grammar school opposite, to lark about the yard, sit on the posts, or dive into a dingy little shop close by, where piles of greasy tarts and cakes lay in the window....*

Miss Jerusha looked up from her seventeenth patchwork quilt, and answered, with a sympathetic glance over the way,—

"If we had enough to go round I'd do it myself, and save these poor deluded dears from the bilious turns that will surely take them down before vacation comes. That fat boy is as yellow as a lemon now, and no wonder, for I've seen him eat half a dozen dreadful turnovers for one lunch."

Both old ladies shook their heads and sighed.... Sitting at the front windows day after day, the old ladies had learned to enjoy watching the boys, who came and went, like bees to a hive, month by month. They had their favorites.... One lame boy was Miss Jerusha's pet, though she never spoke to him, and a tall bright-faced fellow, who rather lorded it over the rest, quite won Miss Hetty's old heart by helping her across the street on a slippery day. They longed to ... feed those who persisted in buying lunch at the dirty bake-shop over the way.

The good souls were famous cooks, and had many books full of all manner of nice receipts, which they seldom used, as they lived simply and saw little company. A certain kind of molasses cookie made by their honored mother,—a renowned housewife in her time,—and eaten by the sisters as children, had a peculiar charm for them. A tin box was always kept full, though they only now and then nibbled one, and preferred to give them away to poor children....

To-day the box was full of fresh cookies, crisp, brown, and sweet; their spicy odor pervaded the room, and the china-closet door stood suggestively open. Miss Hetty's spectacles turned that way, then went back to the busy scene in the street, as if trying to get courage for the deed.

> *Aunt Jo's Scrap-Bag: An Old-Fashioned Thanksgiving, etc.* (1882)
> Louisa May Alcott

Molasses Cookies

1 cup molasses
1/2 cup shortening (butter and
  lard)
1 tablespoon ginger
1 teaspoon soda
2 tablespoons warm milk
2 cups bread flour
1/2 teaspoon salt

Heat molasses to boiling point, add shortening, ginger, soda dissolved in warm milk, and flour. Proceed as for Ginger Snaps.

The Boston Cooking-School Cook Book (1909)
Fannie Farmer

Plain Cookies

3 1/2 cups flour
1 cup sugar
6 ounces butter
3 eggs
1 teaspoon soda
pinch nutmeg or other spice

If richer cookies are desired, take one half pound butter. [Cream butter. Add sugar, eggs, then flour, soda, and spice sifted together. Mix well. Arrange by teaspoonfuls on buttered cookie sheet, 1 inch apart. Bake about 8 minutes at 375˚.]

Six Little Cooks, or, Aunt Jane's Cooking Class (1877)
E. S. Kirkland

S o we decided to join the candy scrape, and in about one minute we were all in the kitchen ready to help, and opening the cupboard doors, and pulling down things from the pantry shelves; and I guess every saucepan in the house was taken out, and all the other pans and tins besides. . . .

In about half an hour we had so many different kinds of candy started that it was pretty hard remembering which was which; and by that time the kitchen looked so mixed up that I was glad the cook was having a holiday. . . .

One or two boys were helping Mercurius stir the molasses-candy mixture in the big preserving-kettle, and he let them do most of the stirring, while he kept dripping little spoonfuls of it in a tumbler of cold water (and on his clothes) to see if it was nearly done.

Several others were helping Josephine Brown, who was about as busy as she could be with "caramels" and "peppermints" and "walnut creams" and "butterscotch" upon her hands. . . .

I had a hard time trying to make the inside of the chocolate drops roll into balls, as they insisted upon all crumbling up, . . . And all the boys who tried to roll them with me got them stuck on to the inside of their hands, and had to eat them up to get them off, so that by the time the insides of the chocolate drops were done there were not many left.

Miss Belladonna: A Child of Today (1897)
Caroline Ticknor

Fondant

2 cups sugar
1 cup cold water
1/4 teaspoon cream of tartar

Place in the kettle two cups (or one pound) of granulated sugar, a cup (or one-half pint) of cold water. When this mixture commences to boil, stir in, lightly, one-fourth teaspoon of cream of tartar, to prevent the syrup becoming sugary. Graining is usually prevented by covering the kettle, so that the steam will wash back into the boiling mass all the accumulations on the sides of the kettle. Boil rapidly, without stirring. Should a crust form on the top, skim off. Test by dropping a little of the syrup into cold water; if it forms a soft ball between the fingers, it is done. Pour quickly into a dish, without scraping the kettle, and allow the mixture to become luke warm. Again skim off any crust there may be on the top. Stir one way, until it looks creamy, then work with the hands until the fondant is fine grain. It will be of finer texture if allowed to stand, covered with a damp cloth, from one to two hours, or longer if convenient. Should the mixture seem rather hard, a little hot water may be added while kneading; if too soft it must be re-boiled. This finished mixture is the foundation for the great variety of cream bon-bons.

Gleaners Pride Cook Book (1897)
Compiled by the Members of the Gleaners' Society of the Congregational Church, Fort Atkinson, Wisconsin

Cocoanut Balls

To a given quantity of the fondant, allow about one third as much desiccated cocoanut, and mix well. Roll the mixture into round balls, and cover with cocoanut.

Gleaners Pride Cook Book (1897)
Compiled by the Members of the Gleaners' Society of the Congregational Church, Fort Atkinson, Wisconsin

Cream Chocolates

2 cups sugar

1/2 cup water

1/2 teaspoon cream of tartar
(mixed with one tablespoon
boiling water)

1 teaspoon vanilla

2 tablespoons powdered sugar

3 ounces baker's chocolate

(optional: nuts or dried fruit)

Put in a saucepan two cups of granulated sugar, one-half cup of cold water, and one-half teaspoonful of cream of tartar dissolved in a little boiling water. Beat all together with a wooden spoon until dissolved. Take spoon out and set over fire. Boil without stirring until it becomes a jelly (try by cooling a little in a spoon.) Take from stove, flavor with vanilla, set in a pan of cold water and beat with a wooden spoon until it is cold when it should be creamy. (If not stiff enough, you can place on the stove and boil a little longer, though they will not be so nice.) Turn out on a marble slab or large platter which has been dusted with powdered sugar. Knead well, then begin molding the pyramids and stand on greased paper to cool. Let stand two or three hours. Then grate one-half bar of chocolate in a bright tin basin, set in a pan of boiling water to melt and keep the pan in the boiling water while using to prevent chocolate from hardening. Sift a molded cream drop, hold in fingers, and with a knife smooth the melted chocolate over it, slide back on greased paper. The syrup may be separated and different flavor added. All kinds of nuts may be used with this cream, and a great variety of candies made. As cream walnuts, dates, figs, almonds, citron, raisins, etc.

Bills of Fare for All Seasons (1896)
Marion Harland

Everton Taffy

1 1/2 pounds brown sugar
6 tablespoons butter
1 1/2 cups cold water
grated peel and juice from 1
    lemon

One and a half pounds brown sugar, three ounces butter, one and a half teacups cold water. Boil all together with the grated rind of one lemon, and when cold add the juice.

Six Little Cooks, or, Aunt Jane's Cooking Class (1877)
E. S. Kirkland

I *t was only the production of the parcel of sugar-plums that brought the least gleam of expression to their vacant eyes. Sugar-plums they seemed to comprehend at once, for all claimed more or less experience in the article, but never had they seen such sugar-plums before! There were burnt-almonds, and kisses, and mint-stick of such vivid white and crimson, and Jackson balls, and cocoanut cakes, and sugar "cows with crumpled horns," and cats that seemed to have pricked up their whiskers at some remarkably nice mice invisible to the company, and little dogs with their tails apparently just out of curl-papers!*

Dear, dear! if their hands had only been larger to hold them! for Philip had been told they were all his, and he must distribute them, which he did liberally; so liberally, that though the boys held out their "double hands," the "sugar-alleys" would run over on to the floor, and the comfits and lozenges slip through their fingers, and then down went the little white heads.

Patient Waiting No Loss; or, The Two Christmas Days (1853)
Alice Bradley Haven

Sugar Plums
Des Dragées Sucrées

2 pounds powdered sugar
water
1 pound any fruit

Sugar Plums, or crystallized fruits, are among the daintiest preparations of the Creole cuisine. They are the real "Bonbons" so highly prized by the Creole girls.

To crystallize fruits or candies in small quantities, take two pounds of the best sugar, and add sufficient water to dissolve it or start it to boiling. Let it boil to a syrup. Place the fruit to be crystallized in a pan, and pour over the syrup. Turn the fruit lightly by shaking the pan till every side is coated, and set to cool. When cool, drain off the syrup and set the pans on their sides, so that remaining particles may be drained off, and every side be coated with the crystallized mixture. It is always best to pour the syrup over the fruit while it is warm, as it takes firmer hold and makes a brighter crystal, but it will not hurt the fruit if the crystal warms them enough to make them very soft, as they will be all right when the syrup and fruits cool. A small batch of crystallized fruit may be prepared at noon, and be ready for a 6 o'clock dining.

Fruits and almond paste bonbons should always be softened by the hot syrup, and it is always best to prepare the fruits two days in advance, when they will be sufficiently soft for a light crystal to form on them.

Chocolate and other bonbons may be crystallized in the same way.

The Picayune Creole Cook Book (1916)
Anonymous Contributors

Meringues

6 egg whites
1/2 pound powdered sugar
(optional: 4 tablespoons ground
    almonds)

Beat to a very solid froth the whites of 6 fresh eggs, and have ready to mix with them half a pound of the best sugar, well dried and sifted. Lay some squares or long strips of writing-paper closely upon a board, which ought to be an inch thick to prevent the meringues from receiving any color from the bottom of the oven. When all is ready for them, stir the sugar to the beaten eggs, and with a table or dessert-spoon lay the mixture on the paper in the form of a half egg; sift sugar quickly over, blow off all that does not adhere, and set the meringues immediately into a moderate oven: the process must be expeditious, or the sugar melting will cause the meringues to spread, instead of retaining their shape. When they are colored a light brown, and are firm to the touch, draw them out, raise them from the paper, and press back the insides with a tea-spoon, or scoop them out, so as to leave space enough to admit some whipped cream or preserve, with which they are to be filled, when cold, before they are served. Put them again into the oven to dry gently, and when they are ready for table fasten them together in the shape of a whole egg, and pile them lightly on a napkin.

Note—4 ounces of pounded almonds may be mixed with the eggs and sugar for these cakes, and any flavor added to them at pleasure. If well made, they are remarkably good and elegant in appearance. They must be fastened together with a little white of egg.

Mrs. Hale's New Cook Book (1857)

Breads, Rolls, Doughnuts, and Flapjacks

*B*ut, beside these mechanical obstacles, there was another difficulty attendant upon baking, of much more serious import, and that was the making of the bread. I scarcely know how I should have conquered this, but for the kind instructions of the excellent old lady whose barrel of rain-water had been so acceptable a letter of introduction. The best of yeast from her own jar was always at my service, and the most patient directions for mixing, kneading, and rising. I had learned in the laboratory that it was a most pernicious thing to suffer bread to pass the stage of saccharine fermentation. ...But theory is one thing, practice another; and though the knowledge I had derived from our lamented professor was by no means useless, yet it did not make my first nor my second loaf of bread as good as that of my neighbor, who had never read a page of chemistry. However, the mysteries of sponge, first mixing, moulding, and second rising, became familiar after a few sour experiences, till I could, with much complacency, set a plate of my own good bread before my husband.

    Life in Prairie Land (1846)
    Eliza Woodson Burhans Farnham

*A*ugust 11 [1885]

Harvest has started. Now there will be no rest for man, woman, or beast until frost which comes, thank heaven, early here. I was nearly beside myself getting dinner for thirteen men, besides carpenters and tinners, with Katie sick in bed and Elsie washing. I baked seventeen loaves of bread today, making seventy-four loaves since last Sunday, not to mention twenty-one pies, and puddings, cakes, and doughnuts.

    A Day at a Time (1985)
    Mary Dodge Woodward

Nineteenth Century Bread

1 pint boiling water
1 pint sweet milk
1 cake yeast (1/2 ounce)
dissolved in 2 tablespoons warm
     water
1 teaspoon salt
3 cups whole wheat flour
3 cups all-purpose flour

Select whole wheat flour, free from outside bran. Pour one pint of boiling water into one pint of sweet milk. When lukewarm, add one compressed yeast cake (one-half ounce) dissolved in two tablespoonfuls of warm water, and one teaspoonful of salt. Mix and stir in sufficient whole wheat flour to make a batter that will drop from a spoon. Beat well, cover and stand in a warm place (75° Fahr.) for three hours until very light. Then stir in more flour, enough to make a soft dough. Knead lightly until the greater part of the stickiness is lost.

This whole wheat bread cannot be made dry like the ordinary white bread, so must be handled quickly and lightly on the board. Now mold it into four or six loaves, according to the size of your pans; place in greased pans. Cover and stand aside again in a warm place for one hour. Bake in a moderately quick oven thirty-five or forty minutes.

Mrs. Rorer's Philadelphia Cook Book (1886)

*O*ne word as to this and similar modes of making bread, so much practised throughout this country. It is my opinion that the sin of bewitching snow-white flour by means of either of those abominations, "salt risin'," "milk emptin's," "bran 'east," or any of their odious compounds, ought to be classed with the turning of grain into whiskey, and both made indictable offences. To those who know of no other means of producing the requisite sponginess in bread than the wholesome hop-yeast of the brewer, I may be allowed to explain the mode to which I have alluded with such hearty reprobation. Here follows the recipe:

To make milk emptin's. Take quantum suf. of good sweet milk—add a teaspoon full of salt, and some water, and set the mixture in a warm place till it ferments, then mix your bread with it; and if you are lucky enough to catch it just in the right moment before the fermentation reaches the putrescent stage, you may make tolerably good rolls, but if you are five minutes too late, you will have to open your doors and windows while your bread is baking.—Verbum sap.

"Salt risin'" is made with water slightly salted and fermented like the other; and becomes putrid rather sooner; and *"bran 'east"* is on the same plan. The consequences of letting these mixtures stand too long will become known to those whom it may concern, when they shall travel through the remoter parts of Michigan; so I shall not dwell upon them here—but I offer my counsel to such of my friends as may be removing westward, to bring with them some form of portable yeast (the old-fashioned dried cakes which mothers and aunts can furnish, are as good as any)—and also full instructions for perpetuating the same; and to plant hops as soon as they get a corner to plant them in.

A New Home—Who'll Follow? (1839)
Caroline Kirkland

Salt-Risen Bread

2 cups flour
1 tablespoon cornmeal
1/2 teaspoon salt

Make into a thin batter:

Set in a warm place to rise. After it has risen, pour into it two quarts of flour, with sufficient warm water to make up a loaf of bread. Work it well, set it to rise again, and when risen sufficiently, bake it.

Another Recipe for the Same

Into a pitcher, put one teacup of milk fresh from the cow, two teacups of boiling water, one tablespoonful of sugar, one teaspoonful of salt. Into this stir thoroughly a little less than a quart of flour. Set the pitcher in a kettle of moderately warm water and keep it at a uniform temperature. Keep a towel fastened over the mouth of the pitcher. Set the kettle in front of the fire to keep the water warm. Let it stand three hours, then beat it up well, after which do not interrupt it. If in two hours it does not begin to rise, put in a large slice of apple. As soon as it rises sufficiently, have ready two quarts of flour, half a tablespoonful of lard and more salt, and make up immediately. Should there not be yeast enough, use warm water. Put into an oven and set before a slow fire to rise, after which bake slowly. The yeast must be made up at seven o'clock in the morning.

Housekeeping in Old Virginia (1879)
Marion Cabell Tyree (ed.)

*W*ellesley College. Wellesley, Mass. Sept 12, 1880.
My Dear Martha,

Thank you very much for your kind letter with Papa's postscript....

Our study hours and recitations are not arranged yet, so I cannot tell you much about that, but I will write when that is appointed. You will be interested to know that our seats at table have been given out alphabetically. There are twenty-five tables, eighteen at each including a teacher who presides....

Mamma wants a bill of fare, so like Papa, I will write what we had for breakfast. Baked beans and brown bread, graham and wheat bread, oatmeal, coffee (coffee twice a week) milk if you choose, water, and fruit, three different kinds of grapes, and apples. Everything is excellent and well and thoroughly cooked. For lunch we have both kinds of bread, cake cookies, cold meat, watermelon, apples, and soup sometimes, milk or water to drink.

> *A Girl of the Eighties* (1931)
> Charlotte Conant

*A*nd I took a little pink china bowl full of good night's milk with a little cream in it, *and a slice or two of my good, sweet graham bread, and put 'em on a little Japan tray with a pretty fringed tidy on it, and a bright silver spoon, and when it was all fixed I took it up to her.*

> *Samantha on Children's Rights* (1909)
> Marietta Holley

Graham Bread

2 1/2 cups hot liquid (water, or
   milk and water)
1/3 cup molasses
1 1/2 teaspoons salt
1 yeast cake dissolved in 1/4
   cup lukewarm water
3 cups flour
3 cups Graham flour (very finely
   milled whole-grain flour)

Prepare and bake as Entire Wheat Bread. Add 1/4 cup sugar or 1/3 cup molasses to 2 cups of scalded milk; cool, and when lukewarm add 1 dissolved yeast cake (in 1/4 cup warm water) to 4 2/3 cups coarse entire wheat flour; beat well, cover, let rise to double its bulk. Beat again, turn into greased pans; let rise, and bake. The bran remaining in sieve after sifting Graham flour should be discarded.

> *The Boston Cooking-School Cook Book* (1909)
> Fannie Farmer

*O*ur bread, to be sure, was the black compound of rye and Indian which the economy of Massachusetts then made the common form, because it was the result of what could be most easily raised on her hard and stony soil; but I can inform all whom it may concern that rye and Indian bread smoking hot, on a cold winter morning, together with savory sausages, pork, and beans, formed a breakfast fit for a king.

Oldtown Folks (1869)
Harriet Beecher Stowe

Thin Indian Bread

2 cups of cornmeal
1 tablespoon lard
1 teaspoon salt
1 cup milk
2 eggs, well-beaten

Mix together two cupfuls of meal, a tablespoonful of lard, and a teaspoonful of salt; scald with boiling water. Thin it with a large cupful of cold milk and two well-beaten eggs. Spread thin on a large buttered pan, and bake till brown in an oven only moderately hot.

The Century Cook Book (1896)
Mary Ronald

Steamed Brown Bread

1 cup cornmeal
2 cups rye flour
1 cup molasses
2 cups milk
1/2 teaspoon baking soda
1/2 teaspoon salt

One cup of Indian meal, two cups of rye, one cup of molasses, two cups of milk, a half-teaspoonful of soda, the same of salt. Stir well together and steam in some of the new "boilers" or "cookers" or "steamers" three hours; taking care that the water does not stop boiling. Add boiling water as the water boils away. If you wish it hot for breakfast, steam the day before, and in the morning set it in the oven for half an hour to form a good crust.

Motherly Talks with Young Housekeepers (1873)
Mrs. Henry W. Beecher

Boston Brown Bread

1 cup cornmeal
1 cup rye flour
1 cup graham flour
2 cups molasses
2 cups milk
1 cup sour milk
3/4 tablespoon baking soda
1 teaspoon salt

One heaping coffee-cup each of corn, rye and Graham meal. The rye meal should be as fine as the Graham, or rye flour may be used. Sift the three kinds together as closely as possible, and beat together thoroughly the two cups New Orleans or Porto Rico molasses, two cups sweet milk, one cup sour milk, one dessert-spoon soda, one tea-spoon salt; pour into a tin form, place in a kettle of cold water, put on and boil four hours. Put on to cook as soon as mixed. It may appear to be too thin, but it is not, as this recipe has never been known to fail. Serve warm, with baked beans or Thanksgiving turkey. The bread should not quite fill the form (or a tin pail with cover will answer), as it must have room to swell. See that the water does not boil up to the top of the form; also take care it does not boil entirely away or stop boiling. To serve it, remove the lid and set it a few moments into the open oven to dry the top, and it will then turn out in perfect shape. This bread can be used as a pudding, and served with a sauce made of thick sour cream, well sweetened and seasoned with nutmeg; or it is good toasted the next day.

Buckeye Cookery (1880)
Estelle Woods Wilcox (ed.)

*Y*ou must imagine the breakfast cheer—but a southern breakfast, if you have never seen one, is beyond your imagination. Corn bread, as yellow, and almost as light, as sponge cake,—rice bread, whiter than any bridal loaf—snow-white hominy and crisp rolls,—omelets, with their sprigs of pungent parsley,—fresh-laid eggs it were a shame to disguise as omelets,—thin slices of pink, delicious ham,—muffins and crumpets,—and many other things that Philip had never seen before, any more than yourselves, I dare say. But I don't think he had a very great appetite, though boys are not generally wanting in this particular.

Patient Waiting No Loss; or, The Two Christmas Days (1853)
Alice Bradley Haven

Soft Corn-Bread

1 tablespoon butter
2 cups hominy or rice, boiled
2 eggs, well-beaten
2 cups milk
1 cup white cornmeal
salt

Mix a tablespoonful of butter with two cupfuls of hot boiled hominy or of rice; add two or three well-beaten eggs, and then add slowly two cupfuls of milk, and lastly a cupful of white cornmeal and a dash of salt. Turn the mixture, which should be of the consistency of pancake batter, into a deep dish, and bake about an hour. Serve it with a spoon from the same dish in which it is baked.

The Century Cook Book (1896)
Mary Ronald

Corn Dodgers

4 cups cornmeal
dash salt
water

One quart of corn meal, a little salt, and water enough to make the batter just stiff enough to make the mixture into cakes with the hands. Bake in a Dutch oven, on tin sheets.

House and Home; or, The Carolina Housewife (1855)
A Lady of Charleston

Sally Lunn

1 pint milk

1 ounce butter

1/2 cup good yeast or 1/4 of a
  compressed cake

1 teaspoon salt

1 teaspoon sugar

3 cups sifted flour

3 eggs, separated

Scald the milk, add to it the butter, and stand on one side until lukewarm; then add the yeast, salt, sugar and flour; beat continuously for five minutes, cover and stand in a warm place for two hours, or until very light. Then beat the eggs separately until very light; add first the yolk and then the whites; stir them in carefully; stand again in a warm place for fifteen minutes; then turn into a greased Turk's head, and bake in a moderately quick oven for forty minutes.

Mrs. Rorer's Philadelphia Cook Book (1886)

Muffins No. 1

2 cups flour

2 teaspoons baking powder

1/2 teaspoon salt

1 cup milk

2 eggs, beaten separately

1 tablespoon butter

Mix thoroughly the baking-powder and salt with the flour. Stir the milk and yolks together; add the butter, melted; then the flour, and lastly fold in the whipped whites. Turn into hot gem-pans, and bake at once in a very hot oven for fifteen to twenty minutes. Serve immediately.

The Century Cook Book (1896)
Mary Ronald

English Muffins

4 cups flour
1 teaspoon salt
1 cake of yeast (0.6 ounce)
1 1/2 cups water

One quart of flour, one teaspoonful of salt, one-third of a cake of compressed yeast, or one-third of a cupful of liquid yeast; one cupful and a half of water. Have the water blood warm. Dissolve the yeast in one-third of a cupful of cold water. Add it and the salt to the warm water, and gradually stir into the flour. Beat the dough thoroughly; cover, and let it rise in a warm place until it is spongy (about five hours). Sprinkle the bread board with flour. Shape the dough into balls about twice the size of an egg, and drop them on the floured board. When all the dough has been shaped, roll the balls into cakes about one-third of an inch thick. Lay these on a warm griddle, which has been lightly greased, and put the griddle on the back of the stove, where there is not much heat. When the cakes have risen a little, draw the griddle forward and cook them slowly, turning often, to keep the flat shape. It will take about twenty minutes for them to rise on the griddle, and fifteen to cook. Tear them apart, butter them, and serve.

Miss Parloa's New Cook Book (1880)

Chloe turned in her chair and stared frankly at the non-committal features under the cap—for I never saw a less vicious-looking person than our new maid.

"Maria?" she stammered.

"Yes, Miss Chloe," said the Terrible Treasure gravely, offering her the rolls.

She makes the most delicious rolls in bewildering variety: wee pointed ones for dinner, crusty brown ones for breakfast and the most mysterious cinnamon-flavored, puffy ones for luncheon.

The Domestic Adventurers (1907)
Josephine Dodge Daskam Bacon

Pocket Books

1 quart milk
1 cup butter or lard
4 tablespoons sugar
2 eggs, well-beaten
flour
1 cup yeast
1 teaspoon baking soda
1 tablespoon milk
butter

Warm one quart new milk, add one cup butter or lard, four tablespoons sugar, and two well-beaten eggs; stir in flour enough to make a moderately stiff sponge, add a small cup of yeast, and set in a warm place to rise, which will take three or four hours; then mix in flour enough to make a soft dough and let rise again. When well risen, dissolve a lump of soda size of a bean in a spoon of milk, work it into the dough and roll into sheets one-half inch in thickness; spread with thin layer of butter, cut into squares, and fold over, pocket-book shape; put on tins or in pans to rise for a little while, when they will be fit for the oven. In summer the sponge can be made up in the morning, and rise in time to make for tea. In cool weather it is best to set it over night.

Buckeye Cookery (1880)
Estelle Woods Wilcox (ed.)

*H*ave you ever eaten or even bitten into a "beat biscuit"? A platter of hot "beat" biscuits for supper, with quince preserves ... or with thick black sugar-house molasses, a culinary alliance fit for bishops and other potentates? This variety of bread was the outcome of a wooden block in a rear yard, of a mallet, also a muscular right arm, which thumped the dough into blisters, and then thumped and thumped again.*

The York Road (1931)
Lizette Woodworth Reese

Maryland Beaten Biscuit

4 cups flour
1 teaspoon salt
1 tablespoon butter
1 cup milk
water

Add a teaspoonful of salt and tablespoonful of butter to a quart of flour. Rub them together, then add a cupful of milk, and, if necessary, a little water, making a stiff dough. Place the dough on a firm table or block, and beat it with a mallet or rolling-pin for fully half an hour, or until it becomes brittle. Spread it half an inch thick; cut it into small circles, and prick each one with a fork. Bake them in a hot oven about twenty minutes.

The Century Cook Book (1896)
Mary Ronald

*"N*ow, we must n't stop again if we can help it," insisted Mrs. Todd at last. "You 'll get tired, mother, and you 'll think the less o' reunions. We can visit along here any day. There, if they ain't frying doughnuts in this next house, too! These are new folks, you know, from over St. George way; they took this old Talcot farm last year. 'T is the best water on the road, and the check-rein 's come undone—yes, we 'd best delay a little and water the horse."*

We stopped, and seeing a party of pleasure-seekers in holiday attire, the thin, anxious mistress of the farmhouse came out with wistful sympathy to hear what news we might have to give. Mrs. Blackett first spied her at the half-closed door, and asked with such cheerful directness if we were trespassing that, after a few words, she went back to her kitchen and reappeared with a plateful of doughnuts.

"Entertainment for man and beast," announced Mrs. Todd with satisfaction. "Why, we've perceived there was new doughnuts all along the road, but you're the first that has treated us."

Our new acquaintance flushed with pleasure, but said nothing.

"They're very nice; you've had good luck with 'em," pronounced Mrs. Todd. "Yes, we've observed there was doughnuts all the way along; if one house is frying all the rest is; 't is so with a great many things."

> *The Country of the Pointed Firs* (1897)
> Sarah Orne Jewett

Doughnuts I

2 1/2 tablespoons butter
1 cup sugar
3 eggs
3 1/2 cups flour
1 cup milk
3 1/2 teaspoons baking powder
1 1/2 teaspoons salt
1/4 teaspoon cinnamon
1/4 teaspoon grated nutmeg

Cream the butter, and add one-half sugar. Beat egg until light, add remaining sugar, and combine mixtures, [add milk]. Add three and one-half cups flour, mixed and sifted with baking powder, salt, and spices; then enough more flour to make dough stiff enough to roll. Toss one-third of mixture on floured board, knead slightly, pat, and roll out to one-fourth inch thickness. Shape with a doughnut cutter, fry in deep fat, take up on a skewer, and drain on brown paper. Add trimmings to one-half remaining mixture, roll, shape, and fry as before; repeat. Doughnuts should come quickly to top of fat, brown on one side, then be turned to brown on the other; avoid turning more than once. The fat must be kept at a uniform temperature. If too cold, doughnuts will absorb fat; if too hot, doughnuts will brown before sufficiently risen.

> *The Boston Cooking-School Cook Book* (1909)
> Fannie Farmer

Raised Doughnuts

4 potatoes
1 cake of compressed yeast
1–2 cups flour
1 pint milk
1 1/2 cups sugar
1/4 cup lard
1/4 teaspoon salt
pinch of nutmeg
pinch of cinnamon
1/2 teaspoon baking soda
    dissolved in 1 tablespoon milk
(optional: raisins, apple-butter)

Peel and boil four good sized potatoes; mash fine, and pour boiling water over them until of the consistency of gruel; let cool, add a yeast cake, and a little flour; let rise till light, then add one pint sweet milk, one and a half cups sugar, one-fourth cup (large measure) lard, a salt-spoon salt, a little nutmeg and cinnamon; stir in flour until stiff, let rise again, then add a half tea-spoon soda dissolved in a little milk, pour out on molding board, mix stiff enough to cut out, and roll to half an inch thickness; cut in long strips two inches wide and divide diagonally into pieces three inches long, set where it is warm, let rise on the board until light, and then fry. These do not cook through as easily as others, and it is safer to drop in one, and, by breaking it open, learn the time required for them to fry. A very nice variation of this recipe may be made as follows: Roll part of the dough about half an inch thick, cut into small biscuit, let rise, and when light, roll down a little, lay a few raisins rolled in cinnamon in the center, wet the edges by dipping the finger in cold water and passing it over them; draw them together and press firmly, and drop them in the hot fat. A tea-spoon of apple-butter or any kind of jam may be used instead of the raisins. When made with raisins, they are the real German "Olly Koeks."

Buckeye Cookery (1880)
Estelle Woods Wilcox (ed.)

*rs. Wilkins was frying flapjacks, and though this is not considered an heroical employment she made it so that day. This was a favorite dish of Lisha's, and she had prepared it as a bait for this cautious fish. To say that the fish rose at once and swallowed the bait, hook and all, but feebly expresses the justice done to the cakes by that long-suffering man. Waiting till he had a tempting pile of the lightest, brownest flapjacks ever seen upon his plate, and was watching an extra big bit of butter melt luxuriously into the warm bosom of the upper one, with a face as benign as if some of the molasses he was trickling over them had been absorbed into his nature, Mrs. Wilkins seized the propitious moment to say impressively:*

"David Sterlin' has enlisted!"

> *Work* (1873)
> Louisa May Alcott

Batter Cakes

2 eggs, separated
1 pint buttermilk
1 cup cornmeal
1/2 cup flour
1/2 teaspoon baking soda
salt

Two eggs beaten separately. Pour into the yolks a pint of buttermilk, then put in two handfuls of meal and one of flour, then the whites of the eggs, half a teaspoonful of soda and a little salt. Fry with very little grease, or with egg shells. Put two spoonfuls of batter to a cake.

> *Housekeeping in Old Virginia* (1879)
> Marion Cabell Tyree (ed.)

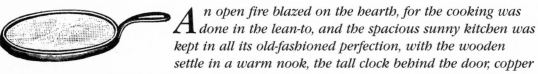*A* n open fire blazed on the hearth, for the cooking was done in the lean-to, and the spacious sunny kitchen was kept in all its old-fashioned perfection, with the wooden settle in a warm nook, the tall clock behind the door, copper and pewter utensils shining on the dresser, old china in the corner closet and a little spinning wheel rescued from the garret by Sophie to adorn the deep window, full of scarlet geraniums, Christmas roses, and white chrysanthemums.*

The young lady, in a checked apron and mob-cap, greeted her friends with a dish of buckwheats in one hand, and a pair of cheeks that proved she had been learning to fry these delectable cakes.

"You do 'keep it up' in earnest, upon my word; and very becoming it is, dear. But won't you ruin your complexion and roughen your hands if you do so much of this new fancy-work?" asked Emily, much amazed at this novel freak.

"I like it, and really believe I've found my proper sphere at last. Domestic life seems so pleasant to me that I feel as if I'd better keep it up for the rest of my life," answered Sophie, making a pretty picture of herself as she cut great slices of brown bread, with the early sunshine touching her happy face.

> *Proverb Stories* (1882)
> Louisa May Alcott

Buckwheat Cakes

4 cups buckwheat meal (flour)
1/2 cup cornmeal
1 teaspoon salt
3 teaspoons yeast
water

Take 1 quart of buckwheat meal, a handful of Indian meal, and a tea-spoonful of salt; mix them with 2 large spoonsful of yeast and sufficient cold water to make a thick batter; beat it well; put it in a warm place to rise, which will take 3 or 4 hours; or, if you mix it at night, let it stand where it is rather cool.

When it is light, bake it on a griddle or in a pan. The griddle must be well buttered, and the cakes are better to be small and thin.

Mrs. Hale's New Cook Book (1852)

Preserves, Jellies, Marmalades, and Pickles

The neighbors generally upheld him in this supposed search. They said he had been "terrible unlucky" in his wives. The first had died in the third year of her marriage. The second had been the best housekeeper for miles around. She put up a greater variety of fruit in cans and more in quantity than any woman ever known in those parts. She had been thrown from a carriage and killed instantly. That was three years ago…

He had come to board with his Aunt Bell. But he hated boarding. He had tried having a housekeeper. But he acknowledged that that arrangement "did not work." Then he tried keeping "bachelor's hall," and that did not work, either. He used to go down cellar and look at the row of fruit cans and think how Ruth had labored with them, and how cross she had been after a morning's work "putting up."

A Widower and Some Spinsters (1899)
Maria Louise Pool

Quinces Preserved Whole

quinces
1 cup sugar
1 cup water

Pare and put them into a saucepan, with the parings at the top, then fill it with hard water, cover it close, set it over a gentle fire till they turn reddish. Let them stand till cold, put them into a clear, thick syrup, boil them for a few minutes; set them on one side till quite cold, boil them again in the same manner. The next day boil them until they look clear. If the syrup is not thick enough, boil it more. When cold, put brandied paper over them. The quinces may be halved or quartered. (Heavy syrup—use 1 cup sugar to 1 cup water.)

The Godey's Lady's Book Receipts (1870)
S. Annie Frost

Lemon Preserves

1 pound lemon peel
1 pound sugar
water

May be made of lemon peel. Put the peel in a preserving kettle and keep covered, while boiling in clear water, till you can run a straw through it. Then throw it into a rich syrup (one pound sugar to one of lemon peel), and boil a long time. Put in a bowl till the next day; then take the syrup (which will be somewhat thin) and boil again till very thick. Pour it over the lemon, and when cold it will be jellied.

Housekeeping in Old Virginia (1879)
Marion Cabell Tyree (ed.)

 *hloe had to superintend the peaches. I had never attempted any, and she had seen her Kentucky aunt do them so many times that she was sure she could.*

Mary, of course, was useless in this connection: she had not reached the subject of preserving in her cooking course and she could do only what she had been taught.

"Preserving, I believe, is very difficult, as well as expensive," she told me. "I will do whatever you tell me, of course, but I could not think of undertaking any responsibility."

"It may require a little experience," I said, "but it is much cheaper to do them at home than to buy them, certainly."

"It would be cheaper still to do without them," she replied doggedly.

> *The Domestic Adventurers* (1907)
> Josephine Dodge Daskam Bacon

Brandied Peaches

3 pounds peaches
3 pounds sugar
1/2 pint water
brandy

The Morris white peaches are the best. Take off the skins with boiling water. To each pound of fruit allow one pound of sugar, and half a pint of water to three pounds of sugar. When the syrup is boiling hot, put in the peaches, and as fast as they cook, take them out carefully and spread on platters. When cool, put them in jars, and fill up these with syrup, using one-half syrup and one-half pale brandy. First-proof alcohol, diluted with an equal quantity of water, can be used instead of brandy, but it is not, of course, so nice.

Miss Parloa's New Cook Book (1880)

Peach Sauce

4 large, mellow peaches
1/2 cup water
1/2 cup sugar
1 cup cream
1 tablespoon cornstarch
2 egg whites

Pare and stone the peaches; put them in a saucepan with the water and sugar, stew until tender, then press them through a colander. Put the cream on to boil in a farina boiler; moisten the corn-starch in a little cold water, and stir into the boiling cream; stir until it thickens; then beat into it the peaches and the whites of the eggs beaten to a stiff froth. Stand in a cold place until very cold.

Apricot Sauce may be made in the same manner, using canned apricots.

Mrs. Rorer's Philadelphia Cook Book (1886)

*S*uch piles of snowy bread and golden cake, such delicate cheeses and puffy biscuits, and such transparencies of rich-coloured preserves, were an undoubted adornment to Mrs. Starling's deal table, and might have been to any table in the world.... Mrs. Starling might smile grimly to herself as she saw her crab-apples and jellies disappear, and the pile of biscuits go down and get heaped up again by Diana's care.

Diana (1877)
Susan Warner

Crab Apple Jelly

1 peck crab apples
water
strained juice of 4 lemons
3/4 pound sugar for each pint of
   juice

Wash and quarter large Siberian crabs, but do not core, cover to the depth of an inch or two with cold water, and cook to a mush; pour into a coarse cotton bag or strainer, and when cool enough, press or squeeze hard, to extract all the juice. Take a piece of fine Swiss muslin or crinoline, wring out of water, spread over a colander placed over a crock, and with a cup dip the juice slowly in, allowing plenty of time to run through; repeat this process twice, rinsing out the muslin frequently. Allow the strained juice of four lemons to a peck of apples, and three quarters of a pound of sugar to each pint of juice. Boil the juice from ten to twenty minutes; while boiling sift in the sugar slowly, stirring constantly, and boil five minutes longer. This is generally sufficient, but it is always safer to "try it," and ascertain whether it will "jelly." This makes a very clear, sparkling jelly.

Buckeye Cookery (1880)
Estelle Woods Wilcox (ed.)

Grape Jelly

grapes
water
2 cups sugar for *each pint* of
  juice

Pick stems from grapes. Put in jar without water and set in kettle of hot water and cook till fruit bursts. Strain in flannel bag and to 1 pint juice add 1 pint sugar. Boil till it begins to jelly and pour in glasses. Cover with paper which has been dipped in brandy, which prevents mould, and set aside in dark place.

The Blue Grass Cook Book (1904)
Minnie C. Fox (ed.)

*F*ired with a housewifely wish to see her store-room stocked with home-made preserves, she undertook to put up her own currant jelly. John was requested to order home a dozen or so of little pots, and an extra quantity of sugar, for their own currants were ripe, and were to be attended to at once. As John firmly believed that "my wife" was equal to anything, and took a natural pride in her skill, he resolved that she should be gratified, and their only crop of fruit laid by in a most pleasing form for winter use. Home came four dozen delightful little pots, half a barrel of sugar, and a small boy to pick the currants for her. With her pretty hair tucked into a little cap, arms bared to the elbow, and a checked apron which had a coquettish look in spite of the bib, the young housewife fell to work, feeling no doubts about her success; for hadn't she seen Hannah do it hundreds of times? The array of pots rather amazed her at first, but John was so fond of jelly, and the nice little jars would look so well on the top shelf, that Meg resolved to fill them all, and spent a long day picking, boiling, straining, and fussing over her jelly. She did her best; she asked advice of Mrs. Cornelius; she racked her brain to remember what Hannah did that she had left undone; she reboiled, resugared, and restrained, but that dreadful stuff wouldn't "jell."*

Little Women (1869)
Louisa May Alcott

Currant Jelly

currants
1 pound sugar to each pint of
   juice

Pick over the fruit, but leave it on the stems. Put it into the preserving kettle, and break it with a ladle or spoon, and when it is hot, squeeze it in a coarse linen bag until you can press out no more juice. Then weigh a pound of sugar to a pint of juice. Sift the sugar, and heat it as hot as possible without dissolving or burning; boil the juice five minutes very fast, and while boiling add the hot sugar, stir it well, and when it has boiled again five minutes, set it off. The time must be strictly observed. Jelly to eat with meat does very well made with brown sugar, but must boil longer.

The Young Housekeeper's Friend (1859)
Mrs. Cornelius

Currant Syrup

3 pounds currants
1 pound raspberries
1 pound cherries
2 pounds sugar to each pint of
   juice

One pint of juice, two pounds of sugar. Mix together three pounds of currants, half white and half red, one pound of raspberries, and one pound of cherries, without the stones. Mash the fruit, and let it stand in a warm place for three or four days, keeping it covered with a coarse cloth or piece of paper with holes pricked in it to keep out any dust or dirt. Filter the juice, add the sugar in powder, finish in the water-bath, and skim it. When cold, put it into bottles, fill them, and cork well.

The Godey's Lady's Book Receipts (1870)
S. Annie Frost

"*I* suppose that means you want peach marmalade and hot biscuits for tea," she said.

"*And some chili-cum-carne first. And a pretty toilette, and a bright face, and smiles, and a song, and general indulgence, and all your sweetness."*

Priscilla's Love Story (1906)
Harriet Prescott Spofford

Peach Marmalade

peaches
3/4 pound sugar to each pound
   of fruit
brandy

Pare the peaches and take out the stones. Fruit which is not dead-ripe or very choice can be used to advantage in this way. For every pound of the prepared peaches allow one dozen "pits," cracked and chopped, and a pound of sugar. Put the fruit and "pits" in a kettle and heat very slowly, breaking it, as it softens, with a wooden ladle. Increase the heat when they are hot all through and boil to pieces, quickly, taking care to stir up from the bottom frequently. Drain out all the syrup that will come away without pressing, before putting in the sugar. Cook to a bright-colored paste, free from hard pieces or lumps, take from the fire, stir in a glass of brandy for every four pounds of fruit, and put up in tumblers. The brandy serves to keep it, and prevents moulding.

Bills of Fare for All Seasons (1896)
Marion Harland

A breakfast indeed, when it appeared! Mrs. Peterkin had mistaken the alphabetical suggestion, and had grasped the idea that the whole alphabet must be represented in one breakfast.

This, therefore, was the bill of fare: Apple-sauce, Bread, Butter, Coffee, Cream, Doughnuts, Eggs, Fishballs, Griddles, Ham, Ice (on butter), Jam, Krout (sour), Lamb-chops, Morning Newspapers, Oatmeal, Pepper, Quince-marmalade, Rolls, Salt, Tea Urn, Veal-pie, Waffles, Yeast-biscuit.

The Peterkin Papers (1887)
Lucretia Hale

Quince Marmalade

1 gallon quinces
3 pounds sugar
1 quart water

To one gallon of quinces three pounds of good loaf sugar. Pare the quinces and cut them in halves, scoop out the cores and the hard strip that unites the core with the string. Put the cores and some of the parings in a saucepan with about a quart of water, put the halves of quinces in a steamer that fits the saucepan, boil them until the quinces are softened by the steam, then mash them with a wooden spoon in a dish and pour the water from the saucepan on them, which is now of a thick glutinous substance. Put them with the sugar in a stewpan or enamelled saucepan, and let them boil for about half an hour, keeping them well stirred.

The Godey's Lady's Book Receipts (1870)
S. Annie Frost

Orange Marmalade

1 pound oranges
3/4 pound sugar
grated rind and juice of 1 lemon
   for each 5 oranges

Allow three-quarters of a pound of sugar to a pound of fruit. Put the peels so that they may be removed in four pieces. Boil these peels in a large quantity of water for two hours, then cut them into fine shreds. While these are boiling, press the inside of the oranges through a sieve fine enough to prevent the seeds and skin from passing through. For every five oranges, add the grated rind and juice of one lemon. Put all into a preserving-kettles with the sugar. When done, the marmalade should be quite thick and solid. Cover closely in little preserving-jars.

Practical Cooking and Dinner Giving (1887)
Mary F. Henderson

G reenfield, Mass. Sept. 28, 1887.
   Dear Martha,

When Miss Annie asks me what I am going to do this winter to occupy my mind I think of the things I already have and find my mind is pretty well occupied as it is.

Take today for instance. This morning I went downtown early and bought peaches and plums and did some other marketing, came home and boiled over the syrup for the sweet pickled pears, put up the plums, and Mamma and I made a large stone jar full of green tomato pickle. Just sniff, and you can smell the nice spicy smell there is all over the house. I called at Grandma's coming up from downtown, put in the ordinary clearing up and a call from Mrs. Packard and you have a sufficiently busy morning. In the afternoon we finished off the tomatoes, then dressed and went to walk round through Orchard St. to Samuel's.

   A Girl of the Eighties (1931)
   Charlotte Conant

Green Tomato Pickles

1 peck green tomatoes
coarse salt
12 large onions
1 1/2 quarts cider vinegar
4 tablespoons white mustard
   seed
4 tablespoons ground mustard
1/2 tablespoon turmeric
1 tablespoon cloves
1 tablespoon allspice
1 tablespoon ginger
1 tablespoon pepper
1 tablespoon cinnamon
1/4 cup salt
1/2 pound brown sugar

One peck of green tomatoes, sliced thin; sprinkle with salt, and let them stand one night; slice twelve onions; put with the tomatoes, and boil in vinegar for two hours, with the following spices: four ounces of white mustard-seed, four of ground mustard, one-half ounce of turmeric, one ounce of cloves, one of allspice, one of ginger, one of pepper, one of cinnamon, one-fourth of a teacupful of salt, and one-half pound of brown sugar.

   Presbyterian Cook Book (1875)
   Ladies of the First Presbyterian Church,
   Dayton, Ohio

Creole Chow Chow

6 onions
1 gallon green tomatoes
1 pint salt
1 gallon wine vinegar
2 cups brown sugar
1 tablespoon cayenne pepper
1 tablespoon black pepper
1 tablespoon turmeric

One gallon of green tomatoes, sliced thin, half dozen silver skin onions, sliced thin, one gallon wine vinegar, two tea-cups of brown sugar, one tablespoonful of cayenne pepper, one tablespoonful black pepper, one tablespoonful of tumerick. Put the onions and tomatoes together in a keg or jar and sprinkle over them one pint of salt and let it so remain twenty-four hours, then drain all the brine off from them over cullender, then put the vinegar to them and add the seasoning, and put to cook on a slow fire, stir to keep from burning. It will take the whole day to cook; you can make any quantity you want, by doubling the quantity of vegetables and seasonings here prescribed, or if you want a less quantity, lessen the proportion, say half the quantity, then you want a half gallon of tomatoes to begin with, and a half of every thing else needed in this chow chow.

What Mrs. Fisher Knows about Old Southern Cooking (1881)

We canned tomatoes yesterday, ripe ones, and I have made some very nice ripe cucumber pickle. It is late now to get things to preserve and pickle. I mean to get some quinces and apples to can together; they are said to be delicious. Some pears would be nice too.

A Girl of the Eighties (1931)
Charlotte Conant

Sliced Cucumber Pickles

1 peck medium sized
  cucumbers
6 onions
salt
1 1/2 quarts vinegar
1/2 pound yellow mustard seed
2 tablespoons cloves
1 tablespoon mace
1 tablespoon turmeric
2 tablespoons brown sugar

Take one peck of medium-sized cucumbers, and one-half dozen onions; slice, and sprinkle with salt; let them lie three or four hours; then drain, and boil in vinegar for ten minutes, with the following spices: one-half pound of yellow mustard-seed, two tablespoonfuls of cloves, one of mace, one of turmeric, and two of brown sugar. Pack in jars, and tie paper closely over them.

Presbyterian Cook Book (1875)
Ladies of the First Presbyterian Church,
Dayton, Ohio

Cucumber Catsup

6 cucumbers
3 onions
1 teaspoon salt
1/2 teaspoon pepper
vinegar

Grate six green cucumbers and three onions. Add to the grated mixture a teaspoonful of salt, and a half a teaspoonful of pepper. Drain off the juice, and, after measuring, throw it away, adding to the catsup the same quantity of vinegar. Mix well and bottle for use.

Cooking and Castle Building (1883)
Emma P. Ewing

Compound Tomato Sauce

1 peck ripe tomatoes
1 cup salt
3 tablespoons ground allspice
1 1/2 tablespoons ground cloves
1 tablespoon black pepper
1 tablespoon cayenne pepper
5 large onions
1 quart vinegar

One peck of ripe tomatoes, cut them in slices and put them in a vessel, and add one tea-cupful of salt to them, two ounces fine allspice, one ounce of fine cloves, one tablespoonful of black pepper and one of cayenne pepper, five large silver skin onions cut up fine, and the whole stand twenty-four hours; mix well together when you set to stand, then put it to cook with one quart of vinegar and let it cook all day; stir it occasionally; it must become thick before it is thoroughly cooked, then strain all skin and studs out of it through a sieve; when cool put in a demijohn, as it will keep better than in bottles when first made.

N. B. If you don't like much pepper use half the quantity, if you like it very hot use double the quantity.

What Mrs. Fisher Knows about Old Southern Cooking (1881)

Festive Occasions and Holidays

Children's parties which began at three in the afternoon and ended in the early dusk, while little ones could see their way home; parties at which there was no "German," only the simplest of dancing ... "mottoes" in sugar horns were the luxurious novelty, caraway cookies the staple, and lemonade the only drink besides pure water.

Bits of Talk about Home Matters (1882)
Helen Hunt Jackson

Caraway Seed Cakes

1 1/2 cups butter
2 1/4 cups sugar
7 cups flour
1 tablespoon caraway seed
1 cup milk
2 tablespoons saleratus (baking powder)

Two pounds of flour, one pound of sugar, three-fourths of a pound of butter, one tablespoonful of caraway seed, half a pint of milk, two tablespoonfuls of saleratus; rub the butter, sugar and flour together thoroughly, then add all the other ingredients, roll it out quite thin, cut with a round cutter, place them on tins, and bake in a moderate oven. This seems a small quantity of milk, but after kneading it a little while it will be found quite sufficient; to add more would spoil them.

Bills of Fare for All Seasons (1896)
Marion Harland

"Your mother and I have had some consultation about our refreshments and other matters," said Mrs. King. "At first we were going to have the good old-fashioned hours of four to eight, but there must be a birthday cake, and that wouldn't be any thing without candles, and the candles won't show by daylight; so, all things considered, as the weather is very hot and the visitors wouldn't want to come out early in the afternoon, the invitations have been made from five to nine."

"The three little ones are going round giving them this morning," said Rose.

"So we will have a regular tea (only there won't be any tea,) at half-past six; and about a quarter before nine we'll have the cake, all lighted up, and some lemonade."

Six Little Cooks, or, Aunt Jane's Cooking Class (1877)
E. S. Kirkland

Birthday Cake

1/2 cup butter
1 1/4 cups brown sugar
yolks of 2 eggs
2/3 cup milk
2 1/4 cups flour
3 1/2 teaspoons baking powder
1 teaspoon orange extract
1 teaspoon vanilla
2 tablespoons sherry
1/2 cup seeded raisins
1/2 cup walnut meats, chopped
1/3 cup currants
2 tablespoons candied orange
   peel, finely cut
whites of 2 eggs

Follow directions for making butter-cake mixtures. Bake in a buttered and floured angel-cake pan in a slow oven, one and one-quarter hours. Cover with white frosting.

Boston Cooking-School Cook Book (1909)
Fannie Farmer

*W*here many guests from out of town are expected, the ceremony usually takes place in the daytime. If the hour fixed is at midday, a substantial collation should be served to those guests invited to the house. To country housewives giving themselves much anxiety about croquettes, pâtés, and other elaborate dishes, it should be said that nothing is better—and nothing more popular with male guests—than good substantial roast beef. At a wedding-breakfast served lately at the country-house of a lady of wealth and position, the bill-of-fare consisted of bouillon in cups, hot roast beef with carrots and green pease, lettuce salad with French dressing, ice-cream, cake, coffee and candies—ending with cigars for the gentlemen and a box of wedding cake laid at each place. Champagne also was served, but it is not now so customary as it was formerly to give wine at a wedding. The bride and groom with their nearest relatives sat at a large oval table, the rest of the guests having their places at small tables in the adjoining rooms or on the wide verandah.

A Handbook of Hospitality for Town and Country (1909)
Florence Hall

Bride's Cake

3/4 pound sugar
1/2 pound butter
1 pound flour
14 egg whites
(optional: 1 1/2 pounds fruit)

Cream sugar and butter together, and stir in them flour and beaten whites, very little at a time; one and a half pounds fruit, prepared and mixed with batter, will make a nice fruit cake.

Housekeeping in Old Virginia (1879)
Marion Cabell Tyree (ed.)

Groom's Cake

1 pound butter
1 pound sugar
10 eggs, separated
2 pounds almonds
1 pound flour
1 pound seeded raisins
1/2 pound citron

Ten eggs beaten separately, one pound butter, one of white sugar, one of flour, two of almonds blanched and chopped fine, one of seeded raisins, half pound citron, shaved fine; beat butter to a cream, add sugar gradually, then the well-beaten yolks; stir all till very light, and add the chopped almonds; beat the whites stiff and add gently with the flour; take a little more flour and sprinkle over the raisins and citron, then put in the cake-pan, first a layer of cake batter, then a layer of raisins and citron, then cake, and so on till all is used, finishing off with a layer of cake. Bake in a moderate oven two hours.

Buckeye Cookery (1880)
Estelle Woods Wilcox (ed.)

Wedding Cake

9 cups butter
10 cups sugar
16 cups flour
5 dozen eggs
7 pounds currants
3 1/2 pounds citron
4 pounds almonds, shelled
7 pounds raisins
1 1/2 pints brandy
2 ounces mace

Nine cupfuls of butter, five pints of sugar, four quarts of flour, five dozen of eggs, seven pounds of currants, three and a half of citron, four of shelled almonds, seven of raisins, one and a half pints of brandy, two ounces of mace. Bake in a moderate oven for two hours or more. This will make eight loaves, which will keep for years.

Miss Parloa's New Cook Book (1880)

O ver the river and through the wood—
Now grandmother's cap I spy!
Hurrah for the fun!
Is the pudding done?
Hurrah for the pumpkin-pie!

"Over the River and Through the Wood," *Flowers for Children* (1844)
Lydia Maria Child

T hanksgiving is almost here, and how shall we celebrate the day? I for one believe in
the old-fashioned Thanksgiving dinner. The following bill of fare may be of use to
some of your readers:

Oyster Soup   Celery, Pepper Sauce
Roast Turkey, with Currant Jelly
Baked Potatoes   Mashed Turnips
Roast Pig   Carrots with Cream   Baked Beans   Chopped Cabbage
Pumpkin Pie   Plum Pudding
Apples   Nuts   Cheese
Tea and Coffee

Dr. Chase's Third Last and Complete Receipt Book (1891)

*T*he furniture of the parlor consisted of a mahogany sideboard and table, a dozen handsome rush-bottomed chairs, a large mirror, the gilt frame covered with green gauze to prevent injury from dust and flies, and on the floor was a substantial, home manufactured carpet, woven in a curious manner and blended with all the colors of the rainbow. Seldom were the junior members of the family allowed the high privilege of stepping on this carpet excepting at the annual festival, and their joy at the approaching feast, was considerably heightened by the knowledge that it would be holden in the best room.

The table, covered with a damask cloth, vieing in whiteness, and nearly equalling in texture, the finest imported, though spun, woven and bleached by Mrs. Romelee's own hand, was now intended for the whole household, every child having a seat on this occasion, and the more the better, it being considered an honor for a man to sit down to his Thanksgiving supper surrounded by a large family. The provision is always sufficient for a multitude, every farmer in the country being, at this season of the year, plentifully supplied, and every one proud of displaying his abundance and prosperity.

The roasted turkey took precedence on this occasion, being placed at the head of the table; and well did it become its lordly station, sending forth the rich odour of its savoury stuffing, and finely covered with the frost of the basting. At the foot of the board a surloin of beef, flanked on either side by a leg of pork and joint of mutton, seemed placed as a bastion to defend innumerable bowls of gravy and plates of vegetables disposed in that quarter. A goose and pair of ducklings occupied side stations on the table, the middle being graced, as it always is on such occasions, by that rich burgomaster of the provisions, called a chicken pie. This pie, which is wholly formed of the choicest parts of fowls, enriched and seasoned with a profusion of butter and pepper, and covered with an excellent puff paste, is, like the celebrated pumpkin pie, an indispensable part of a good and true Yankee Thanksgiving; the size of the pie usually denoting the gratitude of the party who prepares the feast. The one now displayed could never have had many peers.

Northwood; A Tale of New England (1827)
Sarah Josepha Hale

To Roast Goose

1 goose
salt
water
1–1 1/2 cups mashed potatoes
1 tablespoon butter
1 tablespoon bacon, chopped
1 small onion, minced
parsley, thyme, sage

A goose must never be eaten the same day it is killed. If the weather is cold, it should be kept a week before using. Before cooking let it lie several hours in weak salt and water, to remove the strong taste. Then plunge it in boiling water, for five minutes, if old. Fill the goose with a dressing made of:

Mealy Irish potatoes, boiled and mashed fine.

A small lump of butter.

A little salt or fresh pork chopped fine.

A little minced onion.

Parsley, thyme, and a pinch of chopped or powdered sage

Grease with sweet lard or butter. Lay in a pan with the giblets, neck, etc. Pour in two teacups of boiling water, set in a hot oven, and baste frequently. Turn so that every part may be equally browned. Serve with gravy or onion sauce.

The above recipe will answer equally as well for duck.

Housekeeping in Old Virginia (1879)
Marion Cabell Tyree (ed.)

Roast Turkey

For stuffing:
approx. 2 pounds pork sausage
1 egg, beaten
breadcrumbs
1 shallot, shredded
(optional: roasted chestnuts,
    green truffles)

To cook the turkey:
flour
melted butter

To roast a Turkey.—Prepare a stuffing of pork sausage meat, one beaten egg, and a few crumbs of bread; or, if sausages are to served with the turkey, stuffing as for fillet of veal: in either, a little shred shalot is an improvement. Stuff the bird under the breast; dredge it with flour, and put it down to a clear brisk fire; at a moderate distance the first half-hour, but afterwards nearer. Baste with butter; and when the turkey is plumped up, and the steam draws towards the fire, it will be nearly done; then dredge it lightly with flour, and baste it with a little more butter, first melted in the basting-ladle. Serve with gravy in the dish, and bread sauce in a tureen. It may be garnished with sausages, or with fried forcemeat, if veal-stuffing be used. Sometimes the gizzard and liver are dipped into the yolk of an egg, sprinkled with salt and cayenne, and then put under the pinions, before the bird is put to the fire. Chestnuts, stewed in gravy, are likewise eaten with turkey.

A very large turkey will require three hours' roasting; one of eight or ten pounds, two hours; and a small one, an hour and a half.

Roasted chestnuts, grated or sliced, and green truffles, sliced, are excellent additions to the stuffing for turkeys.

Mrs. Hale's New Cook Book (1857)

Roast Turkey

1 12-pound turkey
1 tablespoon soft butter
1 cup boiling water (approx.)

Dressing:
gizzard, heart, and liver
3 cups stale bread
salt and pepper
2 eggs, beaten

Put the gizzard, heart and liver in cold water and boil till tender. When done, chop fine and add stale bread, grated, salt and pepper, sweet herbs, if liked, two eggs well beaten.

Fill the turkey with this dressing, sew the openings, drawing the skin tightly together. Put a little butter over the turkey and lay it upon the grate of your meat-pan. Cover the bottom of the pan well with boiling water. In a half an hour, baste the turkey by pouring over it the gravy that has begun to form in the pan. Repeat this basting every fifteen minutes. In an oven of average temperature, a twelve-pound turkey will require at least three hours' cooking.

Housekeeping in Old Virginia (1879)
Marion Cabell Tyree (ed.)

Cranberry Sauce

2 quarts cranberries
water
4 cups sugar

Stew two quarts cranberries; putting only water enough to keep from sticking to the bottom of the kettle. Keep covered until nearly done, then stir in one quart white sugar, and boil until thick. The color is finer when the sugar is added just before the sauce is done.

Housekeeping in Old Virginia (1879)
Marion Cabell Tyree (ed.)

No wonder! the odour that stole so insidiously to her nostrils was appetizing, for the turkey had plenty of companionship in the oven. A noble chicken-pie flanked his dripping pan on the right; a delicate sucking-pig was drawn up to the left wing; in the rear towered a mountain of roast beef; while the mouth of the oven was choked up with a generous Indian pudding. It was an ovenful worthy of New England, worthy of the day.

Fashion and Famine (1854)
Ann Sophia Stephens

"Ma said, have what we liked, but she did n't expect us to have a real Thanksgiving dinner, because she wont be here to cook it, and we don't know how," began Prue, doubtfully.

"I can roast a turkey and make a pudding as well as anybody, I guess. The pies are all ready, and if we can't boil vegetables and so on, we don't deserve any dinner," cried Tilly, burning to distinguish herself, and bound to enjoy to the utmost her brief authority.

"Yes, yes!" cried all the boys, "let's have a dinner anyway; Ma wont care, and the good victuals will spoil if they aint eaten right up…"

"Did you ever roast a turkey?" asked Roxy, with an air of deep interest.

"Should you darst to try?" said Rhody, in an awe-stricken tone.

"You will see what I can do. Ma said I was to use my jedgment about things, and I'm going to…

"Come, now, if you want roast turkey and onions, plum-puddin' and mince-pie, you'll have to do as I tell you, and be lively about it."…

Now Tilly and Prue were in their glory, and as soon as the breakfast things were out of the way, they prepared for a grand cooking-time…

Both rolled up their sleeves, put on their largest aprons, and got out all the spoons, dishes, pots, and pans they could find, "so as to have everything handy," as Prue said…

"It's the stuffin' that troubles me," said Tilly, rubbing her round elbows as she eyed the immense fowl laid out on a platter before her. "I don't know how much I want, nor what sort of yarbs to put in, and he's so awful big, I'm kind of afraid of him."…

"Well, I'll get the puddin' off my mind fust, for it ought to bile all day. Put the big kettle on, and see that the spit is clean, while I get ready."

Prue obediently tugged away at the crane, with its black hooks, from which hung the iron tea-kettle and three-legged pot; then she settled the long spit in the grooves made for it in the tall andirons, and put the dripping-pan underneath, for in those days meat was roasted as it should be, not baked in ovens.

Meanwhile Tilly attacked the plum-pudding. She felt pretty sure of coming out right, here, for she had seen her mother do it so many times, it looked very easy. So in went suet and fruit; all sorts of spice, to be sure she got the right ones, and brandy instead of wine. But she forgot both sugar and salt, and tied it in the cloth so tightly that it had no room to swell, so it would come out as heavy as lead and as hard as a cannon-ball, if the bag did not burst and spoil it all. Happily unconscious of these mistakes, Tilly popped it into the pot, and proudly watched it bobbing about before she put the cover on and left it to its fate.

> *Aunt Jo's Scrap-Bag: An Old-Fashioned Thanksgiving, etc.* (1882)
> Louisa May Alcott

Plum Pudding

8 eggs
1 pint milk
1 pound grated stale bread or
   1/2 pound flour and 1/2
   pound bread crumbs
1 pound sugar
1 pound suet, chopped fine
1 pound raisins
1 pound currants
2 tablespoons nutmeg
1 tablespoon cinnamon
1 tablespoon mace
1/4 teaspoon salt
1 glass of brandy
1 glass of wine
blanched almonds, sliced, or
   citron
(optional: grated rind of 1 lemon
   or orange)

You must prepare all your ingredients the day before (except beating the eggs) that in the morning you may have nothing to do but to mix them, as the pudding will require six hours to boil.

Beat the eggs very light, then put to them half the milk and beat both together. Stir in gradually the flour and grated bread. Next add the sugar by degrees. Then the suet and fruit alternately. The fruit must be well sprinkled with flour, lest it sink to the bottom. Stir very hard. Then add the spice and liquor, and lastly the remainder of the milk. Stir the whole mixture very well together. If it is not thick enough, add a little more grated bread or flour. If there is too much bread or flour, the pudding will be hard and heavy.

Dip your pudding-cloth into boiling water, shake it out and sprinkle it slightly with flour. Lay it in a pan, and pour the mixture into the cloth. Tie it up carefully, allowing room for the pudding to swell.

Boil it six hours, and turn it carefully out of the cloth.

Before you send it to table, have ready some blanched sweet almonds cut into slips, or some slips of citron, or both. Stick them all over the outside of the pudding.

Eat it with wine, or with a sauce made of drawn butter, wine and nutmeg.

The pudding will be improved if you add to the other ingredients, the grated rind of a large lemon or orange.

Seventy-five Receipts for Pastry, Cakes, and Sweetmeats (1839)
Miss Leslie

Thanksgiving Pie

approx. 3 cups pumpkin filling
2 pie crusts, rolled out
1 recipe for puff paste, for pie
   top
1 egg yolk
1 tablespoon milk
1 teaspoon sugar

Prepare pumpkin pie mixture; take a very large flat pie dish with nearly perpendicular sides, and nearly an inch in depth; the dish should be of earthen or tin and nearly eighteen inches across; rub it over with a bit of sponge dipped in melted butter, cover it with family pie-crust rolled a quarter of an inch thick; cut a strip of paste, the width of a finger, and put it around the inside edge of the pie, then nearly fill it with the pie mixture, and put it in a moderately hot oven; roll some puff paste to less than quarter of an inch thickness, brush it over with the yolk of an egg beaten with a little milk, and a teaspoonful of sugar, then cut it in small stars; cut some of it in strips the width of a finger or a little narrower; when the pie is half baked so that it is firm or set, lay it on the stars, at a little distance from the edge, and the same distance from each other; put a larger one in the centre; of the strips of paste make letters to spell THANKSGIVING; and put six on either side of the star in the centre, midway between that, and those on the edge, so as to form a curve around the centre; cut a strip of the paste half an inch wide and put it around the edge of the pie, then return it to the oven, and let it remain for twenty minutes or more until it is nicely colored and the paste is cooked.

To serve thanksgiving pie after the table is cleared for dessert, place the large pie in the centre, place around it, puddings, jellies, etc., making this the crown of the feast.

The American Lady's System of Cookery
(1860)
Mrs. T. J. Crowen

Forefathers' Dinner

1 quart large white beans
1 pound salt pork
1 corned beef, 6-8 pounds
1 chicken, 4-6 pounds
6 quarts hulled corn
1 turnip
8-10 medium-sized potatoes

Succotash is the great dish in Plymouth at every celebration of Forefathers' Day, December 22. Tradition says it has been made in that town ever since the Pilgrims raised their first corn and beans, and it is supposed they learned to make it from the Indians.

Strangers are rather shy of this peculiar mixture; but it is a favorite dish with the natives, and to this day is made by some families many times through the winter season. Although the dish has never been made by the writer, it has been tested by her in that ancient town many times, and the excellence of the following receipt is unquestionable. It is given in the name of Mrs. Barnabas Churchill, of Plymouth, a lady who has made it for fifty years after the manner handed down through many generations.

One quart of large white beans (not the pea beans); six quarts of hulled corn,—the smutty white Southern corn; six to eight pounds of corned beef, from the second cut of the rattle rand; one pound of salt pork, fat and lean; chicken weighing from four to six pounds; one large white French turnip; eight or ten medium-sized potatoes. Wash the beans, and soak over night in cold water. In the morning put them on in cold soft water. When boiling, change the water, and simmer until soft enough to mash to a pulp and the water is nearly all absorbed. Wash the salt pork and the corned beef, which should be corned only three or four days. Put them on about eight o'clock, in cold water, in a very large kettle, and skim as they begin to boil. Clean, and truss the chicken as for boiling, and put it with the meat about an hour and a quarter before dinner time. Allow a longer time if a fowl be used, and keep plenty of water in the kettle. Two hours before dinner time, put the beans, mashed to a pulp, and the hulled corn into another

Forefathers' Dinner (cont.)

kettle, with some of the fat from the meat in the bottom to keep them from sticking. Take out enough liquor from the meat to cover the corn and beans, and let them simmer where they will not burn. Stir often, and add more liquor if needed. The mixture should be like a thick soup, and the beans should absorb all the liquor, yet it must not be too dry.

Pare, and cut the turnip into inch slices; add it about eleven o'clock, and the potatoes (pared) half an hour later. Take up the chicken as soon as tender, that it may be served whole. Serve the beef and pork together, the chicken, turnip, and potatoes each on separate dishes, and the beans and corn in a tureen. The meat usually salts the mixture sufficiently, and no other seasoning is necessary. Save the water left from the meat, to use in warming the corn and beans the next day, serving the meat cold. This will keep several days in cold weather; and, like many other dishes, it is better the oftener it is warmed over, so there is no objection to making a large quantity. The white Southern corn is considered the only kind suitable for this ancient dinner.

Mrs. Lincoln's Boston Cook Book (1887)

 *A* *Christmas party in a Virginian planter's house! Do you know what that is, reader? I advise those who do not, to set out immediately to the Valley—this is the proper season— and get their limbs dislocated on the detestable roads—the turnpikes are now in a proper trim for such catastrophes— and get picked up and carried into some planter's house, for the sake of being a cherished guest in the coming Christmas holidays, and to have an opportunity of getting over their prejudices against Virginian aristocracy. You who have never visited Virginia . . . have no conception of what Virginian hospitality is. It reminds one of the feudal ages, when the ox was roasted entire, whole pipes of ale broached, (I beg pardon of total abstinence,) and the baron's gates thrown open to all comers—when hospitality, with a flag of truce, arrested for a time all neighborhood feuds. . . . Virginian matrons have an old-fashioned pride in their housekeeping. Why, they have been preparing for Christmas for weeks past! And such stores as they have to prepare from. There is little to be bought—every thing is at hand. The still-room closets furnish the dried fruits, the preserves, the jellies, and even the domestic cordials, wines, and essences—it is for the preparation of these things that the still-room has been set apart. The dairy supplies butter, milk, and cream; the domestic hen-house gives the eggs, large and fresh, the poultry-yard supplies the turkeys, geese, and ducks—they have been fattening for a month past. Then in the meat-house, the great Christmas round of beef has been down in spices for weeks, and the huge Christmas ham is already cured, and the Christmas pies are in fine order. There will be great doings in Virginian country-houses this blessed Christmas. There will be huge bowls of egg-nog brewed before breakfast, and every negro on the plantations will come up to wish a merry Christmas, and to get his glass of brandy, and will come to breakfast with something extremely extra. And then the family will go to church in the old family carriage, and perhaps bring the preacher, if he is a single man, home to dinner. The afternoon will be spent in jollity, and the evening will close with a dancing-party.*

The Mother-in-Law; or, Married in Haste (1875)
Emma D. E. N. Southworth

Savory Sauce for a Roast Goose

1 tablespoon mustard
1/2 teaspoon cayenne pepper
3 tablespoons wine

A tablespoonful of made mustard, half a teaspoonful of Cayenne pepper, and three spoonfuls of port wine. When mixed, pour this (hot) into the body of the goose before sending it up. It wonderfully improves with sage and onions.

The Godey's Lady's Book Receipts (1870)
S. Annie Frost

Giblet Sauce

livers, gizzards, and hearts from
   fowl
1 tablespoon butter
salt and pepper
2 egg yolks

Take the livers, lights, gizzards, and hearts from fowls. Boil very tender, and chop them fine. Make a nice thin drawn-butter, and stir them in; or boil and chop them, and use the water in which they were boiled; season with butter, pepper and salt; beat up the yelks of two eggs, add them, and keep the sauce stirring until it thickens. This sauce is best for roast fowls.

The Godey's Lady's Book Receipts (1870)
S. Annie Frost

Egg Nog

6 eggs, separated
6 tablespoons sugar
1 cup brandy, or 1/2 cup brandy
   and 1/2 cup rum
1 quart milk

Six eggs, a quart of milk, half a pint of brandy, or a gill of brandy and a gill of rum, six table-spoonfuls of sugar; beat the yolks and sugar together, and the whites very hard; mix in the brandy, boil the milk, and pour it into the mixture.

House and Home; or, The Carolina Housewife (1855)
A Lady of Charleston

Tea Punch

3 cups green tea
juice and rind of 6 lemons
1 1/2 pounds sugar
1 quart rum

Three cups of strong green tea (in which put the rind of six lemons, pared very thin), one and one-half pound of sugar, juice of six lemons. Stir together a few minutes, then strain, and lastly add one quart of good rum. Fill the glasses with crushed ice when used. It will keep any length of time bottled. Fine for hot weather.

Housekeeping in Old Virginia (1879)
Marion Cabell Tyree (ed.)

Today I have been employing myself, after reading my letters and eating apples, getting some fruit ready for a fruit cake. I found the baker here would bake cakes very nicely and thought how nice it would be if I could have some Christmas fruit cake baked before I was confined, for I might go along until the last of October, and then it might be a long time before I ever felt strong enough to get things ready for a fruit cake. I had one baked last week and put Mrs. Field in the notion, so both Mrs. Field and I are going to have one baked tomorrow.

An Army Doctor's Wife on the Frontier: Letters from Alaska and the Far West, 1874–1878 (1962)
Emily FitzGerald

Farmer's Fruit Cake

3 cups sour dried apples
2 cups molasses
1 1/2 cups butter
1 cup sugar
4 eggs
1 cup milk
1 teaspoon cloves
1 teaspoon cinnamon
1 teaspoon nutmeg
1 1/2 teaspoons baking soda
3/4 cup wine
4 1/2 cups flour
(optional: 1 cup raisins or
     currants)

Three cupfuls of sour dried-apples soaked overnight in warm water. In the morning drain off the water, chop not too fine, leaving the apple about as large as raisins, then simmer in two cupfuls of molasses two hours or until quite done, that is, until the apple has absorbed all the molasses; one and a half cupfuls of butter well beaten; one of sugar, four eggs, one cupful of sweet milk, one teaspoonful of cloves, one of cinnamon, one of nutmeg, one and a half teaspoonfuls of soda, one wine-glass of wine, four and a half teacupfuls of flour; add one cup raisins or currants, if you please, but roll in flour before putting them to other ingredients; beat all together thoroughly; bake carefully in a well-heated oven. This is excellent to our taste, far better than the richer kind, and more easily digested.

Motherly Talks with Young Housekeepers (1873)
Mrs. Henry W. Beecher

The arrival of Christmas and New Year's brought us our Indian friends again. They had learned something of the observation of these holidays from their French neighbors, and I had been forewarned that I should see the squaws kissing every white man they met. Although not crediting this to its full extent, I could readily believe that they would each expect a present, as a "compliment of the season," so I duly prepared myself with a supply of beads, ribbons, combs, and other trinkets. Knowing them to be fond of dainties, I had also a quantity of crullers and doughnuts made ready the day before, as a treat to them.

To my great surprise and annoyance, only a moderate share of the cakes, the frying of which had been entrusted to Louisa, were brought up to be placed in the "Davis."

"Where are the rest of the cakes, Louisa?"

> *Wau-Bun* (1857)
> Mrs. John H. Kinzie

Crullers

1 tablespoon melted butter
2 heaping tablespoons sugar
1 egg, yolk and white beaten
  separately
1/4 teaspoon cinnamon or mace
1/4 teaspoon salt
flour enough to roll out

Roll the dough one fourth of an inch thick. Cut in rectangular pieces, two and a half by three and a half inches; then make five incisions lengthwise, cutting to within one third of an inch at each end. Take up every other strip, fold each strip together slightly in the middle, and drop them into hot fat.

Mrs. Lincoln's Boston Cook Book (1887)

*B*ut who shall do justice to the dinner, and describe the turkey, and chickens, and with all that endless variety of vegetables which the American soil and climate have contributed to the table, and which, without regard to the French doctrine of courses, were all piled together in jovial abundance upon the smoking board? ... After the meat came the plum-puddings, and then the endless array of pies.

Oldtown Folks (1869)
Harriet Beecher Stowe

"*N*ow we'll make b'lieve we've got ter the dinner—that won't be so hard, 'cause yer 'll have somethin' to do—it's awful bothersome to stan' round an' act stylish.—If they have napkins, Sarah Maud down to Peory may put 'em in their laps, 'n' the rest of ye can tuck 'em in yer necks. Don't eat with yer fingers—don't grab no vittles off one 'nother's plates; don't reach out for nothin', but wait till yer asked, 'n' if you never git asked don't git up and grab it.—Don't spill nothin' on the tablecloth, or like 's not Mis' Bird 'll send yer away from the table—'n' I hope she will if yer do! ... Now we'll try a few things ter see how they'll go! Mr. Clement, do you eat cramb'ry sarse?"

"Bet yer life!" cried Clem, who in the excitement of the moment had not taken in the idea exactly and had mistaken this for an ordinary bosom-of-the-family question.

"Clement McGrill Ruggles, do you mean to tell me that you'd say that to a dinner-party? I 'll give ye one more chance. Mr. Clement, will you take some of the cramb'ry?"

"Yes, marm, thank ye kindly, if you happen ter have any handy."

"Very good, indeed! But they won't give yer two tries to-night,—yer just remember that!— Miss Peory, do you speak for white or dark meat?"

"I ain't perticler as ter color,—anything that nobody else wants will suit me," answered Peory with her best air.

"First-rate! Nobody could speak more genteel than that. Miss Kitty, will you have hard or soft sarse with your pudden?"

"Hard or soft? Oh! A little of both, if you please, an' I 'm much obliged," said Kitty, bowing with decided ease and grace; at which all the other Ruggleses pointed the finger of shame at her, and Peter grunted expressively, that their meaning might not be mistaken.

The Birds' Christmas Carol (1886)
Kate Douglas Wiggin

Hard Sauce

1/3 cup butter
1 cup powdered sugar
1/3 teaspoon lemon extract
2/3 teaspoon vanilla

Cream the butter, add sugar gradually, and flavoring.

> *The Boston Cooking-School Cook Book* (1909)
> Fannie Farmer

Foamy Sauce

1/2 cup butter
1 cup powdered sugar
1 egg
2 tablespoons wine

Cream the butter, add gradually sugar, egg well beaten, and wine; beat while heating over hot water.

> *The Boston Cooking-School Cook Book* (1909)
> Fannie Farmer

Maple Sugar Sauce

1 cup water
1/2 cup maple sugar
4 tablespoons butter
1 teaspoon flour
1 teaspoon nutmeg

Melt over a slow fire, in a small tea-cup of water, half a pint maple sugar; let it simmer, removing all scum; add four table-spoons butter mixed with a level tea-spoon flour, and one of grated nutmeg; boil for a few moments, and serve with boiled puddings. Or, make a "hard sauce" of one table-spoon butter to two of sugar.

> *Buckeye Cookery* (1880)
> Estelle Woods Wilcox (ed.)

Years ago, her uncle Alcibiade, in going away to the war, with the cheerful assurance of youth, had promised his father that he would return to eat Christmas dinner with him. He never returned. And now, of late years, since Monsieur Jean Ba had begun to fail in body and mind, that old, unspoken hope of long ago had come back to live anew in his heart. Every Christmas Day he watched for the coming of Alcibiade....

"But this morning at daylight he was rapping his cane on the back gallery, calling together the negroes. Did they not know it was Christmas Day, an' a great dinner mus' be prepare' for his son Alcibiade, whom he was especting!"

"And so he has mistaken me for his son Alcibiade. It is very unfortunate," said Bartner, sympathetically. He was a good-looking, honest-faced young fellow.

The girl arose, quivering with an inspiration. She approached Bartner, and in her eagerness laid her hand upon his arm.

"Oh, Mr. Bartna, if you will do me a favor! The greates' favor of my life!"

He expressed his absolute readiness.

"Let him believe, jus' for this one Christmas day, that you are his son. Let him have that Christmas dinner with Alcibiade, that he has been longing for so many year'."...

The dining-room was at the end of the house, with windows opening upon the side and back galleries. There was a high, simply carved wooden mantelpiece, bearing a wide, slanting, old-fashioned mirror that reflected the table and its occupants. The table was laden with an overabundance. Monsieur Jean Ba sat at one end, Esmée at the other, and Bartner at the side....

Monsieur Jean Ba ate little, but that little greedily and rapidly; then he stayed in rapt contemplation of his guest.

"You will notice, Alcibiade, the flavor of the turkey," he said. "It is dressed with pecans; those big ones from the tree down on the bayou. I had them gathered expressly." The delicate and rich flavor of the nut was indeed very perceptible....

Bartner was distracted with admiration; whether for this beautiful and consoling faith, or its charming votary, was not quite clear to him.

Every now and then Monsieur Jean Ba would call out, "Alcibiade, mon fils!" and Bartner would hasten to his side. Sometimes the old man had forgotten what he wanted to say. Once it was to ask if the salad had been to his liking, or if he would, perhaps, not have preferred the turkey aux truffes.

Bayou Folk (1894)
Kate Chopin

Chestnut Sauce
Sauce aux Marrons

1 pint large chestnuts
1 tablespoon flour
1 tablespoon butter
1 pint boiling stock
salt and pepper

Roast the chestnuts, and peal and mash them very fine. Make a Brown Roux with the flour and butter, and add the boiling stock. Let it boil for about five minutes, and add the mashed chestnuts, stirring constantly, and seasoning to taste. Let it boil for two minutes, take off, and serve hot, with Broiled Dindonneau (turkey chicks). This is a great Creole dish, and is considered a more recherché and delicate one. The sauce may also be served with Roast Turkey.

The Picayune Creole Cook Book (1916)
Anonymous Contributors

Bibliography of Sources

First editions have been used whenever available; some titles are only available in reprint form.

Alcott, Louisa May, 1832-1888. *Aunt Jo's Scrap Bag: An Old-Fashioned Thanksgiving, etc.* Boston: Roberts Brothers, 1882.

———.*Eight Cousins: or, The Aunt-Hill.* Boston: Roberts Brothers, 1875.

———.*Little Men: Life at Plumfield With Jo's Boys.* Boston: Roberts Brothers, 1871.

———.*Little Women, or, Meg, Jo, Beth and Amy.* Part Second. Boston: Roberts Brothers, 1869.

———.*Proverb Stories.* Boston: Roberts Brothers, 1882.

———.*Silver Pitchers.* Boston: Roberts Brothers, 1876.

———.*Work.* Boston: Roberts Brothers, 1873.

Bacon, Josephine Dodge Daskam, 1876-1961. *The Domestic Adventurers.* New York: Scribner's, 1907.

Beach, Minta Asha Philips. *My Walk from New York to Chicago.* New York: Beach Publishing Co., [1912]

Beecher, Catharine Esther, 1800-1878, and Harriet Beecher Stowe. *The American Woman's Home, or, Principles of Domestic Science.* New York: J. B. Ford; Chicago: J. A. Stoddart, 1869.

Beecher, Henry Ward, Mrs. 1813-1897. *Motherly Talks with Young Housekeepers.* New York: J. B. Ford, 1873.

Bowen, Sue Petigru, 1824-1875. *Lily: A Novel.* New York: Harper, 1855.

Campbell, Helen, 1839-1918. *The Easiest Way in Housekeeping and Cooking.* Boston: Roberts Brothers, 1893.

Capital City Cook Book, by the Women's Guild of Grace Church, Madison, Wisconsin, 1883; rpt. New York: Promontory Press, 1974.

Champney, Elizabeth W., 1850-1922. *Three Vassar Girls in Russia and Turkey.* Boston: Estes and Lauriat, c1889.

Chase, A. W., 1817-1885. *Dr. Chase's Third Last and Complete Receipt Book.* Detroit; Windsor, Ont.: F. B. Dickerson, 1891, c1887.

Child, Lydia Maria Francis, 1802-1880. *The American Frugal Housewife.* New York: S. S. and W. Wood, 1838, c1835.

———."Over the River and Through the Wood," in *Flowers for Children.* New York; Boston: J. H. Francis, 1844-46.

Chopin, Kate, 1851-1904. *The Awakening*. Chicago: H. S. Stone, 1899.
———. *Bayou Folk.* Boston; New York: 1894.

Christian, Eugene, and Mrs. Christian (Mollie Griswold). *Uncooked Foods and How to Use Them.* New York: Health Culture Co., 1904.

Conant, Charlotte Howard, 1862-1925. *A Girl of the Eighties at College and at Home.* Boston; New York: Houghton, Mifflin, c1931.

Cooke, Rose Terry, 1827-1892. *Root-Bound and Other Sketches.* Boston: Congregational Sunday-School and Publishing Society, 1885. Rpt. Ridgewood, N.J.: Gregg Press, 1968.

Coolidge, Susan, 1835-1905. *A Little Country Girl.* Boston: Roberts Brothers, 1885.
———. *Two Girls.* Boston: Little, Brown, 1900.

Cornelius, Mary Hooker, 1796-1880. *The Young Housekeeper's Friend.* Boston: Taggard and Chase, 1859.

Cousin Alice: see Haven, Alice B.

Crowen, Mrs. T. J. *The American Lady's System of Cookery: Comprising Every Variety of Information for Ordinary and Holiday Occasions.* New York: T. J. Crowen, 1860.

Diaz, Abby Morton, 1821-1904. *The Schoolmaster's Trunk.* Boston: James R. Osgood, 1874.

Dickinson, Emily, 1830-1886. *Letters of Emily Dickinson.* Edited by Mabel Loomis Todd. New York: Harper, 1931.

Ewing, Emma P., b. 1838. *Cooking and Castle Building.* Chicago: Fairbanks, Palmer, 1883.

Farmer, Fannie Merritt, 1857-1915. *The Boston Cooking-School Cook Book.* Boston: Little, Brown, 1909.

Farnham, Eliza Woodson Burhans, 1815-1864. *Life in Prairie Land.* New York: Harper, 1846.

Fern, Fanny, 1811-1872. *Caper-Sauce: A Volume of Chit-chat about Men, Women, and Things.* New York: G. W. Carleton, 1872.
———. *Ruth Hall: A Domestic Tale of the Present Time.* New York: Masons Brothers, 1855. Rpt. New Brunswick, N.J.: Rutgers University Press, 1986.
———. *Shadows and Sunbeams: Being a Second Series of Fern Leaves from Fanny's Portfolio.* London: W. S. Orr, 1854.

Fisher, Abby. *What Mrs. Fisher Knows about Old Southern Cooking, Soups, Pickles, Preserves, Etc.* San Francisco: Women's Cooperative Printing Office, 1881.

FitzGerald, Emily McCorkle, 1850-1912. *An Army Doctor's Wife on the Frontier: Letters from Alaska and the Far West, 1874-1878.* Edited by Abe Laufe. Pittsburgh: University of Pittsburgh Press, 1962.

Fox, Minnie C. *The Blue Grass Cook Book.* New York: Fox, Duffield, 1904.

Frost, S. Annie. *The Godey's Lady's Book Receipts and Household Hints.* Philadelphia: Evans, Stoddart, 1870.

Gleaners Pride Cook Book. Compiled by the Members of the Gleaners' Society of the Congregational Church, Fort Atkinson, Wisconsin, 1897.

Hale, Lucretia Peabody, 1820-1900. *The Last of the Peterkins, With Others of Their Kin.* Boston: Roberts Brothers, 1886.
——. *Mrs. Hale's New Cook Book.* Philadelphia: T. B. Peterson, [c1857]
——. *The Peterkin Papers.* Boston: Ticknor, 1887.

Hale, Sarah Josepha Buell, 1788-1879. *Northwood; A Tale of New England.* Boston: Bowles and Dearborn, 1827.

Hall, Florence Howe, 1845-1922. *A Handbook of Hospitality for Town and Country.* Boston: D. Estes, 1909.

Harland, Marion, 1830-1922. *Bills of Fare for All Seasons of the Year,* with *Food for the Hungry.* Philadelphia: P. W. Ziegler, 1896.
——. *Breakfast, Luncheon and Tea.* New York: Scribner's, 1875.

Haven, Alice B. *Patient Waiting No Loss; or, The Two Christmas Days.* New York: D. Appleton, 1853.

Henderson, Mary F. *Practical Cooking and Dinner Giving.* New York: Harper, 1887.

Hentz, Caroline Lee, 1800-1856. *Helen and Arthur: or, Miss Thusa's Spinning Wheel.* Philadelphia: A. Hart, 1853.
——. *The Planter's Northern Bride.* Philadelphia: A. Hart, 1854.

Holley, Marietta, 1836-1926. *Samantha at the World's Fair, By Josiah Allen's Wife.* New York: Funk and Wagnalls, 1893.
——. *Samantha on Children's Rights.* New York: G. W. Dillingham, c1909.

Holloway, Laura C. *The Hearthstone; or, Life at Home: A Household Manual.* Chicago: Smith and Miller, 1886.

House and Home; or, The Carolina Housewife. By a Lady of Charleston. Charleston, S.C.: J. Russell, 1855.

Humphrey, Mary A. *The Squatter Sovereign, or, Kansas in the '50's.* Chicago: Coburn and Newman, 1883.

Jackson, Helen Hunt, 1830-1885. *Bits of Talk about Home Matters.* Boston: Roberts Brothers, 1882.

Jackson, Nannie Stillwell. *Vinegar Pie and Chicken Bread: A Woman's Diary of Life in the Rural South, 1890-1891.* Fayetteville: University of Arkansas Press, 1982.

Jewett, Sarah Orne, 1849-1909. *The Country of the Pointed Firs.* Cambridge, Mass.: Houghton, Mifflin, 1897.

Johnson, Mrs. F. Barrett. *Rocks and Romance.* New York; Chicago: J. S. Ogilvie, c1889.

King, Caroline Howard, 1822-1909. *When I Lived in Salem, 1822-1866.* Brattleboro, Vt: Stephen Daye Press, 1937.

Kinzie, Mrs. John H., 1806-1870. *Wau-Bun: The "Early Day" in the Northwest.* Chicago: D. B. Cooke, 1857.

Kirkland, Caroline M., 1801-1864. *A New Home—Who'll Follow? Or, Glimpses of Western Life.* New York: C. S. Francis, 1839.

Kirkland, Elizabeth Stansbury. *Six Little Cooks, or, Aunt Jane's Cooking Class.* Chicago: Jansen, McClurg, 1877.

Larcom, Lucy, 1824-1893. *A New England Girlhood.* Boston: Houghton, Mifflin, 1889.

Lee, Hannah Farnham, 1780-1865. *The Harcourts: Illustrating the Benefit of Retrenchment and Reform.* New York: S. Colman, 1837.

Leslie, Eliza, 1787-1858. *Seventy-five Receipts for Pastry, Cakes, and Sweetmeats.* Boston: Munroe and Francis, 1839, c1827.

Lincoln, Mary Johnson, 1844-1921. *Mrs. Lincoln's Boston Cook Book.* Boston: Roberts Brothers, 1887.

May, Sophie, 1833-1906. *Uncle Barney's Fortune (Little Pitcher Stories, v.3).* Boston: Henry A. Young and Co., 1867.

Miller, Elizabeth Smith, 1822-1911. *In the Kitchen.* Boston: Lee and Shepard, 1875.

Owen, Catherine, d. 1889. *Ten Dollars Enough: Keeping House Well on Ten Dollars a Week; How It Has Been Done; How It May Be Done Again.* Boston: Houghton, Mifflin, 1887.

Parloa, Maria, 1843-1909. *Miss Parloa's New Cook Book: A Guide to Marketing and Cooking.* Boston: Estes and Lauriat, 1880.

The Picayune Creole Cook Book. New Orleans: The Times-Picayune, 1916.

Pool, Maria Louise, 1841-1898. *In a Dike Shanty.* Chicago: Stone and Kimball, 1896.
____. *A Widower and Some Spinsters.* Chicago: H. S. Stone, 1899.

Potter, Eliza. *A Hairdresser's Experience in High Life.* Cincinnati: Published for the Author, 1859. Rpt. New York: Oxford University Press, 1991.

Pratt, Ella Farman. *The Cooking Club of Tu-Whit Hollow.* Boston: D. Lothrop, 1876.

The Presbyterian Cook Book, compiled by the Ladies of the First Presbyterian Church, Dayton, Ohio. Dayton: John H. Thomas and Co., 1875.

Randolph, Mary, 1762-1828. *The Virginia Housewife; or, Methodical Cook.* Baltimore: Plaskitt and Cugle, 1839, c1828.

Reed, Myrtle, 1874-1911. *At the Sign of the Jack O' Lantern.* New York: Putnam, c1905.

Reese, Lizette Woodworth, 1856-1935. *A Victorian Village: Reminiscences of Other Days.* New York: Farrar and Rinehart, 1929.
———. *The York Road.* New York: Farrar and Rinehart, 1931.

Ronald, Mary, 1844-1903. *The Century Cook Book.* New York: The Century Co., 1896.

Rorer, Sarah Tyson, 1849-1937. *Mrs. Rorer's Philadelphia Cook Book: A Manual of Home Economies.* Philadelphia: Arnold, 1886.

Sedgwick, Catharine Maria, 1789-1867. *Live and Let Live, or Domestic Service Illustrated.* New York: Harper, 1837.

Sigourney, Lydia Howard, 1791-1865. *The Girls' Reading Book,* in *Prose and Poetry for Schools.* New York: J. Orville Taylor, 1839.
———. *Lucy Howard's Journal.* New York: Harper, 1858.

Southworth, E. D. E. N. (Emma Dorothy Eliza Newitte), 1819-1899. *The Mother-in-Law, or, Married in Haste.* New York: F. M. Lupton, c1875.

Spofford, Harriet Prescott, 1835-1921. *Priscilla's Love Story.* New York: Duffield, 1906, c1898.

Stephens, Ann Sophia, 1810-1886. *Fashion and Famine.* New York: Bunce, 1854.

Stowe, Harriet Beecher, 1811-1896. *Oldtown Folks.* Boston: Fields, Osgood, 1869.
———. *We and Our Neighbors; or, The Records of an Unfashionable Street.* New York: J. B. Ford, 1875.

Summerville, Amelia. *Why Be Fat?* New York: Frederick A. Stokes, 1916.

Thaxter, Celia, 1835-1894. *Letters of Celia Thaxter.* Edited by her friends A. F. and R. L. Boston: Houghton, Mifflin, 1895.

Ticknor, Caroline, 1866-1937. *Miss Belladonna: A Child of Today.* Boston: Little, Brown, 1897.

Tyree, Marion Cabell, ed. *Housekeeping in Old Virginia.* Louisville, Ky: John P. Morton and Co., 1879.

Warner, Susan, 1819-1885. *Diana.* New York: Putnam, 1877.
———. *The Wide, Wide World.* New York: Putnam, 1852.

Wheaton, Emily. *The Russells in Chicago.* Boston: L. C. Page, 1902.

Whitcher, Frances M., 1814-1852. *The Widow Bedott's Papers.* New York: J. B. Millar, 1884.

Wiggin, Kate Douglas, 1856-1923. *The Birds' Christmas Carol.* Boston: Houghton, 1886.
———, ed. *A Book of Dorcas Dishes.* Cambridge, Mass.: Privately Printed, 1911.
———. *Mother Carey's Chickens.* Boston: Houghton, Mifflin, 1911.
———. *My Garden of Memory.* Boston: Houghton, Mifflin, 1923.

Wilcox, Estelle Woods, ed. *Buckeye Cookery and Practical Housekeeping.* Minneapolis: Buckeye, 1880.

Wolf, Emma, 1865-1952. *Heirs of Yesterday.* Chicago: A. C. McClurg, 1900.

Woodward, Mary Dodge, 1826-1890. "A Day at a Time," in *A Day at a Time: The Diary Literature of American Women from 1764 to the Present,* edited by Margo Culley. New York: Feminist Press, 1985.

Woolson, Constance Fenimore, 1840-1894. *Anne.* New York: Harper, 1882.

Wright, Julia McNair, 1840-1903, comp. *Food for the Hungry: A Complete Manual of Household Duties.* Philadelphia: P. W. Ziegler, 1896.

Index